ALL EQUAL UNDER THE ACT?

- a practical guide to the Children Act 1989 for social workers

by

Sheila Macdonald

Typesetting and design by Diana Seaney
The Pankhurst Press,
60-62 Nelson Street,
Manchester M13 9WP
Tel. 061 273 5673

Printed by
Repro City Ltd.
20 Willow Street
London EC2

Reprinted December 1991

Sub-editor Melba Wilson.

Price: £8.00
(including postage).

Payment with orders (payable to "NISW") to:

Race Equality Unit (REU)
Personal Social Services,
NISW (North), 5th Floor,
National Deposit House,
1 Eastgate,
Leeds,
West Yorkshire
LS2 7LY.

Tel. (0532) 428777. Fax (0532) 341958

or

Race Equality Unit (REU)
Personal Social Services,
NISW, Mary Ward House,
5-7 Tavistock Place,
London
WC1H 9SS.

Tel. (071) 387 9681

CONTENTS

045146

CHAPTER ONE
SOCIAL WORK AND THE HISTORY OF DISCRIMINATION

Contents

CHAPTER TWO
SOCIAL WORK AGENCIES AND THE COMMUNITY

CHAPTER THREE
SOCIAL WORK AGENCIES AND FAMILIES

Contents

Contents

THE STEERING GROUP

Celia Atherton	-	Family Rights Group
Virginia Burton	-	National Council of Voluntary Child Care Organisations
Ratna Dutt	-	Race Equality Unit, National Institute for Social Work
Gillian Loughran	-	LBTC - Training for Care
Suzanne Lyn-Cook	-	Social Services Team, Local Government Management Board (previously LGTB)
Marcia Richards	-	Black Issues Project, British Agencies for Adoption and Fostering

About the author

Sheila Macdonald is a social worker and former guardian *ad litem*. She is currently providing training and consultancy on the Children Act to local authorities and other organisations.

ACKNOWLEDGEMENTS

The author and steering group gratefully acknowledge the contributions made by many people who generously agreed to discuss ideas with us, or offer comments on the draft of the book.

Members of the discussion groups

Barbara Abbott............................Albert Kennedy Trust
J. Alert...Black and in Care
Ann Crowley.................................Children's Society, Cardiff
Pam Donnellan.............................Assistant Director of Social Services, L.B. Haringey
Perlita Harris...............................Black and in Care
Mary Hayes..................................Social worker, Independent Adoption Society
Paul Knight...................................Director of Social Services, L.B. Waltham Forest
Mary MacLeod.............................Polytechnic of North London
John Metcalfe...............................Department of Health
Kate Parsons................................Training Officer, Sandwell S.S.D.
Jenny Pearce.................................Middlesex Polytechnic
Roy Pearson.................................Social Services Inspectorate
S. Raymond..................................Black and in Care
Phillipa Russell...........................Voluntary Council for Handicapped Children
Mary Ryan....................................Family Rights Group
Arunda Sanyal.............................Senior social worker, L.B. Waltham Forest
Pratiba Shenton...........................Children Act Implementation Team, Leicestershire S.S.D.
Roger Smith..................................Children's Society, London
Winifred Stone.............................National Council of Voluntary Child Care Organisations
Marie Walsh.................................Social worker, L.B. Hillingdon
Allan Watson................................Family Service Unit
Michael Watson...........................Social worker, L.B. Hammersmith & Fulham
Nicola Wyld..................................Children's Legal Centre

I

The Steering Group

Readers

Sindee Bass	Social worker, L.B. Waltham Forest
Dermot Casey	Social worker, L.B. Camden
Kalpana Chauhan	London Boroughs Disability Resource Team
Nikki Davies	Social worker, L.B. Waltham Forest
Families in Care	Newcastle upon Tyne
Families in Care	Norfolk
Richard Hughes	Berkshire County Council
Adele Jones	National Institute for Social Work (North)
Maria Lui	LBTC - Training for Care
Sue Mc Caskie	Senior social worker, Hertfordshire S.S.D.
Peter Riches	LBTC - Training for Care
Ian Rush and colleagues	Burymetro S.S.D.
Phillipa Russell	Voluntary Council for Handicapped Children
Julia Smith	Local Government Management Board
Vanessa Strang	Social worker, L.B. Hammersmith and Fulham
Sue Toole	Senior social worker, L.B. Westminster
Gary Vaux	Welfare Rights Officer, L.B. Camden
Chris Wood	Local Government Management Board

Special Thanks

In particular, we would like to extend our thanks to the following:

L.G.M.B - for funding this project.

Sheena Wheeler, L.G.M.B Social Services Team and Jan Bryan, Race Equality Unit - for administrative support.

Information team, L.G.M.B. - for helpful advice and assistance.

Leonie Jordan, solicitor - for assistance with referencing the text.

INTRODUCTION

In February 1990 the Social Services Team of the Local Government Training Board (now Local Government Management Board) brought together a group of professionals to look at and write about the equality issues in the Children Act. The Group consisted of three black and three white women all of whom are able bodied. After the formalising of the group the responsibility of the publication including the financial responsibility was transferred to the Race Equality Unit. The Group now calling itself the 'Steering Group' then commissioned Sheila Macdonald, a member of the Steering Group, to be the writer of the publication.

The main focus of the publication is race and disability although connections are made and examples given, of discriminatory practice which happens on a wider range of issues such as gender, class, disability, sexual identity and poverty. The rationale to focus on disability, although by no means the only reason, is primarily due to the new sections of the Act which will have a significant effect on children with disability. The focus on race similarly is partly due to the Act's expectation that due consideration will be given to race, religion, culture and language. I will elaborate further on the main rationale for focussing on race and racism.

Getting the book ready and deciding on priorities posed a challenge to the Steering Group and highlighted some major issues around working together in a mixed black and white group. I want to use part of this introduction to share some of the issues the Steering Group had to deal with in producing this book as it relates to our experience of working together in a black and white alliance. It is important for white professionals to acknowledge that practice with black children and their families needs to be understood in the context of black and white relationships, which further needs to be understood within the context of racism.

Racism which affects practice with black children/families also affects working relationships between black and white professionals.

The Steering Group had to come to terms with this and learn to acknowledge our differences in perceptions and our realities. White members came to realise that challenge and confrontation by black members was not a personal attack but a challenge of issues and that the challenge was necessary if practice with black children is to improve.

One important issue confronting the group in the initial stage was around personal priorities and perspectives. Although there was general agreement that racism as an oppression would need to be addressed, individual members felt other oppressions needed equal attention. Through debate it was agreed that racism would be the major focus of the book not least because for the first time in children's legislation there is an expectation in the Act that race, culture and language be given due consideration. The main rationale to focus on race and racism, however, is because we believe that dealing with racism necessitates addressing other forms of oppression. Racism affects the lives of all black people regardless of gender, class, sexuality, age or disability. What form it takes may differ according to who you are and where you are but it will affect you nonetheless. Similarly racism will be experienced by all black people from white people whether the white people be men or women, old or young, rich or poor, working class or middle/upper class, able bodied or disabled, gay or lesbian.

The decision to focus on race and disability posed a dilemma for the Steering Group as the writer of the publication is white and able bodied and although members' of the Steering Group is mixed in relation to black and white we, too, are all able bodied. We do not mean to suggest that white people cannot write sensitively on issues of racism or that able bodied people cannot write on issues of disability. It needs to be acknowledged, however, that white people are in a

Introduction I

position of power in relation to black people and that experiences of black people can be and often are, misrepresented by white people. Many black professionals are also aware that views on racism expressed by them are less acceptable and palatable than those expressed by white professionals and are no longer prepared to have their ideas and views interpreted and expressed by white professionals. Often able bodied people feel they are in a position to interpret the needs of people with disabilities and feel they have a right to speak on behalf of people with disabilities. To try and redress the situation the Steering Group agreed that two scene setting articles would be written, one from a black perspective and the other from a black disability perspective. Bandana Ahmad sets the scene from a black perspective and Nasa Begum sets the scene from a black disability perspective. The rest of the book, although informed and helped by black members in the Steering Group and elsewhere, and informed, too, by people with disabilities, must be seen to be from a perspective that Sheila as a white able bodied woman brings.

The experience of working together in a mixed group has meant the recognition that our perceptions as black and white people of situations may, and often will vary, but that debate around the differences can result in positive outcomes as in the production of a publication in this instance. There is a recognition that power differentials exist in a black and white relationship in all settings and to deny that is denying reality for black people. There is an acknowledgement that black professionals and black led organisations will be marginalised and bypassed and that white professionals must always be ready to challenge this.

In hindsight the group recognises that it would have been vital for the group membership to include a member with a disability. This has raised issues for all of us able-bodied women, which we hope will influence our own practice.

We hope the sharing of this experience is useful for you and that you will be mindful of the issues when working in a mixed black and white alliance.

We hope, too, that the book will give you ideas and tools to begin addressing glaring bad practice that continues with oppressed groups of people in this society. There needs to be a recognition that we live in a society which does not treat all human beings living within or outside of this society equally. We live in a society with a past history of slavery, imperialism and exploitation. Social work professionals constantly see the effects of oppression and discrimination on the lives of the people that they are paid to serve. Evidence tells us that white professionals have done not nearly enough to question the discrimination and oppression that destroys the lives of black children.

It is important for professionals to remember the context within which they work with children and their families. To forget the context means denying the reality of day to day existence for children whose lives are affected by racism, by their disabilities and by the worse effects of poverty.

We hope this book helps you to begin to challenge and confront some of the institutional and personal beliefs and actions that involve all professionals in the cycle of discrimination.

This Act with its expectations that due consideration must be given to race, religion, culture and language will only be successful if it is interpreted and implemented positively by agencies and staff within agencies. There must be a willingness and commitment to ensure that the welfare of the black child is seen in the context of his/her race, religion, culture and language. This further necessitates looking at the religion, culture and language of the black child in the context of racism and the way racism views the culture, language and religion of black people. If we fail to give paramount consideration to these four factors then work with black people will continue to be one of control rather than care. Similarly, if children are not seen in their own right but only in relation to their disabilities, only oppressive practice with black and white children with disabilities will continue.

If social workers are to be perceived as agents of social change as much as agents of social control then issues of equality and rights must be firmly fixed on the agenda for policy and practice.

Ratna Dutt
Race Equality Unit

Introduction

GLOSSARY

RACE

Unacceptable categorisation of peoples in biological terms constructed by white pseudo-scientists * to aid the justification of the systematic oppression of black people and create an ideology of racism. For the sake of practical advantage it is now commonly used to denote black and white people.

RACISM

A belief that black people are inferior to white people in relation to their culture, religion, intellect, beliefs, lifestyles. An ideology developed by white people backed by pseudo-scientists, historians, literary persons, religious and missionary bodies, academics, politicians and media, supporting the belief that physical criteria determines intellectual and other abilities.

BLACK

The word is used here to define people who suffer racism because of their skin colour. In the context of British society, we refer to those of African, Caribbean and South East Asian origin.

MINORITY ETHNIC

Belonging to a cultural, racial or religious group that is numerically smaller than the predominant white protestant majority power base in the United Kingdom. This includes groups visible on the basis of their skin colour, as well as others such as Irish, Jewish, Polish, Turkish and Travelling peoples. Belonging can come either through personal identification with a group or through the allocation by others or individuals to it.

ETHNICITY

Refers to individuals' identification with a group sharing some or all of the following traits: customs, lifestyles, religion, language, nationality. In the context of this society, the "racial factor" influences individuals' definition of their own ethnicity (such as black/ Asian, black/ Caribbean). It is important to remember that white people also belong to ethnic groups.

WHITE

People who do not experience racism (that is, as a result of their skin colour).

EUROCENTRIC

Looking at, exclusively valuing and intepreting the world through the eyes and experiences of white Europeans. This includes, for example, the presentation and intepretation of historical events; defining of "correct" methods of child rearing and organising family life; seeing Europe as the centre of the world.

SAME RACE

This is included because of its common usage to describe the placement of black children with black substitute families. Within this, it is about placing black children with families of the same or similar ethnic background.

* refs: Jean-Joseph Virey 1774-1847; David Hume 1742-1745; Robert Knox 1850; Linnaeus 1735.

CULTURE

An identity which everyone has, based on a number of factors, such as: memories, ethnic identity, family attitudes to child rearing, class, money, religious or other celebrations, division of family roles according to gender or age. Cultures are neither superior nor inferior to each other. They are constantly evolving for individuals and communities.

DISABLED

Having a physical, emotional or learning impediment that requires the provision of specific facilities to enable the individual to fully participate in, contribute to, and benefit from, both their personal life and the full rights and responsibilities of citizenship, insofar as they choose to do so.

ABLE BODIED

Having no physical, emotional or learning impediment requiring the provision of specific facilities to enable the individual to participate, contribute and benefit as they choose. Many people with disabilities prefer the term "able-bodied" or the generic term "differently- abled".

ABLISM

People who experience discrimination as a result of having a physical, emotional or learning impediment. This can be institutional or personal discrimination and is based on the belief that to be able-bodied is to be superior.

SEXUALITY

A sense of self as a sexual being which may be expressed in a number of ways. In the course of their lives, adults may choose to be sexually active or celibate.

SEXUAL IDENTITY

An expression of sexuality, by which adults define their sexual identity. This may be lesbian, gay, heterosexual or bisexual.

HETEROSEXISM

A belief that heterosexual behaviour and relationships are the norm and that therefore other sexual behaviour and relationships are abnormal and deviant.

HOMOPHOBIA

Discrimination based on heterosexist beliefs.Both personal and institutional, it is supported by legislation affecting family life, employment and immigration rights and civil liberties. In this context, it affects all lesbian and gay social workers, adult and young adult clients, prospective carers and colleagues from other agencies.

SEXISM

The personal and institutional differentiation of power and status between the sexes which limit opportunities for girls and women both as service users and staff.

Introduction

*Setting the
Context:
Race and
The Children
Act 1989*

If legislation alone could bring about equality and justice, and amend the discriminatory outcome of social work policies and practices, then it could have been argued that considerations of race, culture, religion and language of black children should have been an integral part of social work practice, since at least 1976. For 1976 was the year of the revitalised Race Relations Act, imposing clear duties on local authorities, hence social services as well, "to eliminate unlawful racial discrimination, and to promote equality of opportunity and good relations between persons of different racial groups" (Section 71 (a) and (b)), and introducing specific duties to ensure that services are non-discriminatory "as regards their quality or the manner in which or the terms on which" they are provided (Section 20). In 1991, fifteen years on, there is little evidence of the social work profession using the Race Relations Act 1976 to rid itself of its suppressive use of resources and oppressive forces. The Race Relations Act 1976 has not really been able to make the necessary link between the quality of social work for black children and their families and the equality in social work with black children and their families.

Undoubtedly, the Children Act 1989 is one of the first far reaching pieces of child care legislation in Britain, with a comprehensive legal framework to protect and promote the interest and welfare of children. In the midst of the overwhelming evidence of "culturally insensitive" and "colour blind" social work practice, inclusion of children's racial origin, ethnic background, religion and language in the Act and making it unlawful to ignore these four crucial aspects, is a positive move in the right direction. However, like the Race Relations Act 1976, the Children Act 1989 may end up with little or no impact in promoting the welfare and protecting the interest of the black child, if the interest and welfare of the black child are left to the rhetoric of the Act and not transferred into social work action.

With or without the legal and statutory obligations, social work has a moral and professional duty to ensure that black children and their families receive appropriate and equal services. In order to fulfil the legal obligations of the Children Act 1989, social workers and allied professionals, in particular white social workers and allied professionals, need to examine whether their moral and professional duties towards black families and their children have really been realised and to what extent. Evidence suggests that social work values and knowledge, which are based on eurocentric perceptions, social work methods and approaches, which are derived from white definitions of what is "normal" or "deviant", social work intervention and action which are designed to operate with white families, more often than not, work against the interest and protection of the black child. It is neither an accident nor a coincidence that in the main, controlling tenets of social work still dominate its professional relationships with black children and their families. The dominance of social work control is a manifestation of social work perception of black children, which is influenced by pathological and dysfunctional assumptions about black families. In this context, social work finds justification in "rescuing" the black child from his/her "unsatisfactory" family circumstances and "disadvantaged" family conditions. Inherent in this social work intervention is the validation of an alternative childcare approach, which is "better" than the child care in the black family, and the alternative and better childcare model is inevitably the westernised white model. So the black child's "racial" or "cultural" origin and "religious" or "linguistic" background remain outside the social work consideration during its intervention and planning. Even when the considerations are made, they are not usually made with positive references. On the contrary, references to "race, culture, religion and language" reinforce the "cultural deficit" perspective of social work, perpetuating negative stereotypes of black families. Or, "race, culture, religion and language" are used to disguise the so called "culturally sensitive " approach in non-intervention of social work, victimising the black child needing social work protection. Examples of how black children have been denied protection from sexual abuse (eg. incest), because social workers are too sensitive to intervene, in case incest is culturally accepted in black culture, are not few and far between (Ahmad 1989). It is essential that social work and allied professions make an urgent shift from their racist practices and eliminate discriminatory outcomes from their professionalism. Otherwise they may find themselves, not just falling short of fufilling their moral duties and professional obligations, but also breaching the Children Act 1989.

For black children and their families, the implementation of the Children Act 1989 is not just about taking note of "race, culture, religion and language", and paying partial attention to only those sections of the Act which refer to these four areas. If the Children Act 1989 is for the benefit of all children, whether black or white, then it must follow that ALL sections of the Act relate to black children(Ahmad 1990). If "race, culture, religion and language" have specific implications for black and minority ethnic children, then it must also follow that these four aspects have implications for ALL sections of the Act. The question is, how are the social work and allied professions going to identify the implications in their practices. More importantly, how are they going to interpret the legal requirements of the Act in their practices.

It is perhaps regrettable that the court's duty to make the welfare of the child its paramount consideration is not accompanied by a specific requirement to include race, religion, culture and language in its deliberations (Section 1). This duty is only laid on local authorities and others providing day care or accommodation for children, at which point they must give these issues due consideration (Section 22 (5) (c), Sec-

tion 61 (3) (c), Section 64 (3) (c), Section 74 (6). This has opened up the possibilities for different interpretations of what are "due" considerations as opposed to what are "paramount" considerations. Social work and allied professions must ensure that their interpretations do not act against the interest and welfare of the black child. They must realise that their definitions of and criteria for "due" or "paramount" considerations are crucial in either condoning racist practices or condemning them. They must recognise that whatever their definitions are and however varied the criteria for "due consideration" may be, the fact is that the welfare of black children can neither be promoted, nor be protected fully without giving paramount consideration to their racial and cultural background (Ahmad 1990).

In addition to the "due" consideration v. "paramount" consideration, child care and child protection workers need to be aware of their understanding and ability to assess the "individual" needs of black children, which is stressed in the Children Act 1989. It is highly probable that some workers may not perceive the black child's racial, cultural, religious and linguistic needs as "individual" needs, or may not incorporate the four areas of needs in the assessment of individual needs. Yet the fact is that an individual, whether an adult or a child, does not exist in a vacuum, nor do the social or other problems, faced by the individual. Not to take account of racial, cultural, relious and linguistic needs of a black child within his or her individual needs tantamounts to extracting the child out of his/her social reality. No social problems can be tackled or resolved outside the social reality. It is imperative that the black child's individual needs are met in the context of the child's racial and cultural needs. Otherwise social work may continue to delude itself in pretending to protect and promote the interest and welfare of the black child, while the impact of their practice may be quite the opposite.

Generally the legislative framework aims

Introduction

Setting the Context: Race and The Children Act 1989

to set a standard for practice which must be maintained. If a standard of practice falls below the objectives of the legal duties, then it is considered to be in breach of the law. It is worth remembering that the Children Act 1989 within its central and continuing theme of welfare of the child and legal obligations to "promote" and "protect" welfare, has set out a standard for child care and child protection work, which can be applied as minimum requirements. Consequently, the minimum requirements do not preclude bettering the standard beyond the requirements of the Act. No profession is worth its salt if it stops developing or keeps on operating with minimum standards. There is no other area of social work which demands higher standards of performance than work with black children and their families. The realisation of the Children Act 1989 for the black child is more than staying above the bottom line.

The Children Act 1989 provides an exciting and challenging opportunity to reform child care work and radicalise child protection work with black children and their families. Potential for maximising positive use of the Act in enhancing anti-racist social work policy and practice should not be underestimated. Implementation of the Act and application of its legal requirements to the benefit of black children and their families depend much on the professionals and their institutions, who are responsible to abide by the Act. This book illustrates how those responsibilities can be carried out. In so doing, it places the onus of anti-racist child care and child protection work on the professionals. For too long black families and their children have carried the burden of unequal social work. It is about time they stopped carrying this burden. Equality in social work is long overdue, as is "All Equal Under the Act?"

REFERENCES

1. **B. Ahmad -** Protecting black children from abuse - Social Work today - 8 June 1989

2. **B. Ahmad -** Black Perspectives In Social Work - Venture Press - 1990.

3. Ibid no. 2.

Bandana Ahmad,
Director, Race Equality Unit,
National Institute of Social Work

Introduction

I

Services for people with disabilities are primarily provided by three main sources: health, social services and voluntary organisations. They have developed on the principle that a range of fairly uniform provision can service the needs and wishes of the black and minority ethnic communities. Therefore the different and diverse needs of a multi-racial community of disabled people have to a large extent been left unaddressed.

Limited progress has been made in terms of incorporating a race dimension into policies and practices relating to children and families, and is virtually non-existent in the area of disability.

For many people with disabilities and their families the key to a full and dignified life in the community is access to appropriate and sensitive services. However, black and minority ethnic families have persistently been left to struggle with practical, financial and emotional difficulties with little or no support.

A number of surveys in London, Bradford and Birmingham have clearly demonstrated that there is extremely low take up of welfare services from the black and minority ethnic communities. Communication, access to information, transport, religious and cultural insensitivity, institutional and individual racism are to name but a few of the hurdles that black and minority ethnic people with disabilities and their carers have to confront.

For most children with disabilities the major defining characteristic in their lives is their disability. The disability is allowed to take centre stage, and their needs, wishes and aspirations as children are pushed to one side. The problem is compounded for many black and minority ethnic children because their disability becomes the focus of attention, and their needs as a black and minority ethnic child are overlooked or placed on a

back shelf. The failure to recognise and acknowledge the additional dimension of race often means that for many black and minority ethnic children with disabilities a significant part of their identity and needs are ignored and unmet. One man describes his experiences of growing up as a black disabled person (Disability Now, March 1991).

"Day by day my awareness of race came second to my awareness of disability, because it seemed the most practical way to deal with my life."

Disability and race, along with gender and sexual identity, cannot be regarded as separate and discrete categories. It is the combined and cumulative effect of these different dimensions which influences the lives of individuals. The needs of black and minority ethnic children with disabilities are the same as the needs of other children. The additional dimension of disability and race, however, necessitates a different response or creates additional requirements. It is crucial that at the centre of all policy and practice initiatives the needs of black and minority ethnic children with disabilities are considered in terms of both race and disability.

The Children Act heralds a major advance in recognising the needs, wishes and aspirations of children with disabilities as children in their own right. It provides a framework for moving towards integrating the needs of children with disabilities into mainstream service provision. Its most significant and striking impact, however, will be the fact that attention is drawn to addressing race, religion, culture and language as a key component in determining the welfare of the child. The assessment of black and minority ethnic children with disabilities should not simply concentrate on the practical issues arising from the person's disabilities but a holistic approach must be developed to encompass all the different dimensions. For example, the es-

Introduction

*Setting the
Context:
Disability and
The Children
Act 1989*

tablishment of registers of 'children in need' must ensure that ethnic monitoring, gender and disability are collected and cross-tabulated appropriately. All local authorities should have readily available data about its local black and minority ethnic disabled population. However, care will need to be taken to ensure that information is collected sensitively and does not infringe individual civil rights.

At a time when major service providers are restructuring the design and delivery of services, it is crucial that the needs and wishes of black and minority ethnic people with disabilities and their families are placed at the centre of all discussions and developments and not left on the margin.

The Children Act 1989 and the National Health Service and Community Care Act 1990 represent a radical restructuring in social welfare policies and practices in Britain. The Government White Paper 'Caring for People' states (1 .3):

"The two programmes are consistent and complementary and, taken together, set a fresh agenda and new challenges for social services for the new decade".

The philosophy underlying both Acts is one of providing services within the 'community' or 'family' home according to individual needs. Common principles embodied in the Acts are:

i)   Parental/user involvement

ii)   Needs-led services

iii)   Stimulation of private and voluntary (independent) sector

iv)   Cost effectiveness, value for money and public accountability

v)   Multi-disciplinary, inter-agency working

vi)   Consideration of race, religion, culture and language

The N.H.S. and Community Care Act is not explicit on the issues of race, religion, culture and language - nevertheless it should still be the responsibility of policy makers and practitioners at all levels to ensure that services such as respite care (and many others) do not merely cater for the indigenous white population, but reflect the specific needs of the black and minority ethnic community.

The two Acts provide a framework for standards of good practice and quality assurance. Some of the specific measures which have been made mandatory are:

a)   Assessments of need with regular reviews

b)   Clear and explicit planning

c)   Published information on services, eligibility criteria

d)   Complaints procedures and user representation

e)   Minimum intervention

f)   Practical support to carers/parents

g)   Service agreements and charges

h)   Inter-agency working

i)   Provision of day/respite/preventative services

j)   Register of potential users

k)   Registration and inspection

l)   Quality control and assurance

The fundamental difference between the two Acts primarily rests on the arrangements for funding and the client group that they endeavour to serve. Clearly an Act targeted at children and their families has a somewhat more paternalistic role than one where the State tries to act as a facilitator and enabler. In order to ensure that the needs of children with disabilities and their families are properly served the principles, aims and duties of both Acts must be fully integrated into policies and practice.

The two Acts could provide a major breakthrough for children with disabilities and their families. The heavy emphasis on assessment of need will not provide any comfort or support to black and minority ethnic families unless radical measures are taken to challenge practitioners' stereotyped views about black people with disabilities. A holistic approach must be adopted to ensure a full and thorough assessment in which the child and family play a full part. This needs to be followed through with financial support and services identified by the child and family as necessary. Unless a range of flexible and appropriate services are readily available to black and minority ethnic children with disabilities and their families, the gains will be few. This is probably the most alarming and worrying aspect, particularly as the black and minority ethnic independent sector is not sufficiently developed to provide a range of competitively priced services. Consequently, many black and minority ethnic children may have to continue to make do with the charitable works of major affluent white institutions like the Spastics Society, Royal National Institute for the Blind, Royal National Institute for the Deaf and many more.

The Children Act and the Community Care Act could provide the keystones for a range of effective, efficient, and sensitive services. But without a political, practical and financial commitment, particularly in terms of the black and ethnic minority communities, it will continue to be like so much that has gone before - a vessel of empty promises - not worth the paper it is published on.

Nasa Begum,
Senior Research and Development Officer (Race and Disability), London Borough of Waltham Forest.

April 1991

Introduction

Setting the Context: Disability and The Children Act 1989

CHAPTER ONE
SOCIAL WORK AND THE HISTORY
OF DISCRIMINATION

I. CHILDREN AND THEIR FAMILIES IN BRITAIN

The Children Act, implemented in October 1991, will affect the lives of thousands of children and their families in this country for very many years. A proportion of those children will be known to social service, education and health departments, probation, the police and voluntary organisations, others will be involved in private arrangements and disagreements between the adults in their lives which require the courts' ratification or intervention.

All these families, no matter what their private circumstances, share a common experience - the combined influence on them of British history, politics, economic and social policies. They also share daily preoccupations with getting through life in the best way they can, including their fears, hopes and worries about money, health, education, jobs and relationships.

Depending on who they are, however, these common experiences and preoccupations will have a very different effect and level of influence on each individual family. It is important, therefore, to understand some of how this happens, in order to appreciate the significance of the Children Act. This is because the Act is more than just a collection of new duties and powers to be absorbed into current practice, but also represents a new philosophy and approach to child welfare.

So what are some of the national and international issues which are going to affect our family lives in the 1990s?

1. Britain as a multi-ethnic society

British society has, for many hundreds of years, included a diversity of peoples from races and cultures around the world. Over the centuries, this small group of islands has been constantly settled by groups of migrants. Some of these came to conquer, others for refuge, still others for work and some to be with those already here. This much we have in common with other countries. What is distinctive about Britain, and other equally ambitious nations, however, was the development of empire. This established a relationship of exploitation and subjugation with other countries. It also brought about an ensuing legacy of dependence, hatred and struggle. Now, as this century draws to a close, Britain appears confused about its status, and exhibits the symptoms of a national disease concerning its colonialist inheritance. Whilst continuing to trade on an international reputation as a superpower, developed

largely on the strength of other countries' resources, our society has turned against the people of those countries with a vengeance, increasingly refusing them permission to live, even temporarily, in the relative safety and security of Great Britain, and behaving with extraordinary vindictiveness if they do.

For almost 100 years, Britain has been legally enforcing this turning away of settlers on the basis of their race, *(see glossary)* culture *(see glossary)* or religion, starting with the Jews in 1905. This legacy of hostility which has been particularly, but not exclusively, directed at black people, pervades every aspect of our lives - political, economic, social and personal. Black citizens have been well aware for many years that white social institutions oppress and suppress them by the disproportionate extent to which they are labelled as "mad" or "bad", are locked

up or locked away and lose their children into local authority care. This knowledge is now becoming well enough established to have provoked legislators into beginning to make provisions to outlaw such discrimination, for example the Race Relations Act. Other measures have been aimed at forcing the courts to reconsider their sentencing behaviour (suggested amendment to the Criminal Justice Bill 1990); and in child care - including duties in the Children Act to ensure that practitioners take positive account of children's racial origin, cultural background, language and religion.

2. Britain in Europe

Britain begins the 1990s with a mixture of curiosity, apathy and misgiving on the brink of fuller participation in Europe, but with a growing awareness that the process of integration with the Continent is irreversible. As 1992 approaches, there are many who view its advent with trepidation because of the wider implications of this attachment to Europe. As barriers fall within the community, and there is greater mobility and access to jobs, education, health, housing and welfare services amongst member countries, the barriers to outsider nations will increase. It is likely that poor, white Europeans will be encouraged to travel further than ever in search of work; poor, black non-Europeans will be actively barred from doing the same thing. Immigration laws, which are always increasingly restrictive, will become more specific in an effort to force non-Europeans to remain outside. Simultaneously, access to other rich white nations is also likely to be reduced.

3. Individuals and the State

We move into the 1990s assessing the cumulative effects of recent international and domestic, social and economic policies on individuals, families, our sense of community and our relationships with the State. What we have witnessed from central government is a determination to reduce collective power, responsibility and accountability in socio-economic terms. This is seen,

particularly, in attempts to detach the welfare system, schools and health services from publicly-accountable authorities. At the same time there has been a contradictory shift to greater central government control over organisations such as local authorities and trades unions. There has been increasing stress laid on individual responsibility and self-determination, the latter having been turned on its head and become an absolute and private responsibility to make our lives work, no matter what our economic and personal circumstances. Nowhere is this more apparent than in the ill-fated attempts to introduce the community charge, or poll tax, which represented a superficial attempt to remind all of us of our rights and responsibilities as citizens. It was met with a groundswell of outrage at its unfairness and intrusive nature. In particular, the tax discriminated against both poor and black households. It coincided with a period during which there has been a growing population of families living in poverty (1), and widening gaps between rich and poor (2). Collective responsibility for their situation has not been forthcoming and attempts to find solutions continues to be placed firmly in the hands of individuals and charities. "To be poor is to endure conditional citizenship" wrote Peter Golding in Ruth Lister's analysis of the subject (3).

Failure to see any problem in terms of a collective responsibility for cause, outcome and solution has filtered into social policy and social work practice. It is noticeable when, for instance, a single parent's ability to care for her child is measured not in terms of women's employment prospects and child care options, but in the context of her lack of responsibility in not providing a father for her child; or when young people leaving public care are labelled as voluntarily homeless because grossly inadequate resources do not enable them to establish themselves as independent adults.

4. The acceptable face of families

In the last few years, the concept of "the family" has become a sacred institution, in defence of which political weapons must be drawn.

In September 1990, at the annual conference of the Directors of Social Services, the Leader of the Opposition, Rt.Hon. Neil Kinnock, said:

"..the quality of family life and the quality of our society are indivisible....employment of women with families is...both a positive choice and a necessity...there is..a clear link between family poverty and family breakdown..."

It should be made clear at the outset, however, that for some national leaders, only certain kinds of families are eligible for moral and practical support and approbation. Successive Conservative governments have made strenuous efforts - through legal and economic sanctions and extensive media coverage - to:

i) convince the British public that the so-called traditional family lifestyle is the safe, healthy and above all, right way to raise our children:

This view was echoed by the Lord Chancellor, Lord Mackay, when he said:

"The integrity and independence of the family is the basic building block of a free and democratic society and the need to defend it should be clearly perceivable in law. Accordingly, unless there is evidence that a child is being or is likely to be positively harmed because of a failure in the family, the State, whether in the guise of a local authority or the court, should not interfere." (4)

ii) determine which kinds of families are not acceptable at all:

The Local Government Act 1988, section 28 states:

"A local authority shall not...(b) promote the teaching in any maintained school of the acceptability of homosexuality as a pretended family relationship."

iii) restrict the ability of some families to live together at all:

The Immigration Act 1988, for example, abolished a long-standing right of male Commonwealth citizens to have their wives and children join them in Britain.

iv) force some women to reveal and/or remain involved with their children's fathers through reliance on them for income maintenance:

The 1991 Child Support Bill creates a Child Support Agency from 1992. It is designed to force women to get maintenance from their chidren's fathers, on penalty, for some, of reduced benefit. The Bill is aimed at ensuring that the cost of children is borne by both natural parents and not, where the mother is on benefit, by the State as a whole. The Secretary of State for Social Security has described it as "a natural progression from the Children Act 1989".

v) remind everyone that the decision to have children is a personal and lifelong commitment and one with which the sState will not assist financially:

Measures include: child benefit levels which are not maintained; social security changes remove entitlement to single item grants and replace them with a discretionary system based mainly on loans; British maternity and paternity leave is amongst the worst in Europe; minimal choice and availability of child care facilities for those without substantial incomes; benefit cuts to teenagers; help with child care costs for working single parents removed from the income

Chapter 1

Social Work & the History of Discrimination

support system.

There is no doubt that the Government has decided to pay serious attention to the changing nature of family life in Britain, (see Chapter 3 p48) particularly as it relates to women's child- rearing behaviour and economic independence. It is also clear that the media is continuing to dominate with an obstinately-held view both about what families are like, and what they should be like, despite overwhelming evidence to the contrary on both counts:

FACT BITE:	25% of children are now born outside marriage (5)
FACT BITE:	of married women with children, 50% are employed (6)
FACT BITE:	only 8% of the male workforce supports a non-earning wife and two children (7)
FACT BITE:	in 1987, 14% of dependent children lived in lone-parent families (8).

Social work educators, policy-makers and practitioners need to be aware of the influence of these laws, language and inaccurate theories on us all. To discuss "the family" without acknowledging a wide variety of equally valid and positive models in our society (in which adults and children thrive) is to collude with perpetuating the current belief system and its practices. (See Chapter 3 for further discussion about different family lifestyles.)

All the above points to the fact that our common experience is not a shared experience. It is highly charged with meaning and power, which for some people has a beneficial effect, and for others is deeply hostile and damaging. Recognition that some of our laws, systems and behaviour are unfair and harmful to some groups of people has led to the passing of further laws to make discrimination illegal. Some of these are familiar:
Race Relations Act (1976), Sex Discrimination Act (1975), Disabled Persons Representations Act (1988), Equal Pay Act (1970)

We have to recognise, however, that discrimination does not only happen to a small group of unfortunate people, perpetrated by another group, whilst others get on with their lives, treating each other as equals. Discrimination is not just about numbers. It is about power, and how it is organised through the structures and individuals in our society. A closer look at the legislation and its implementation would reveal that although the majority of us are protected by it, in many cases it fails to work effectively.

Throughout this guide, we want to offer some ideas about how practitioners, working with children and their families and being conscious of how these facts and experiences contribute to the current system of oppression in Britain, can develop their personal strategies to fight discrimination within the framework offered by the Children Act.

II. SOCIAL WORK WITH CHILDREN AND THEIR FAMILIES

In focussing ourselves on the task we set ourselves - which is to assess the Children Act in terms of how it enables us to adopt and carry out positive equality policies - it may be helpful to think about some issues affecting children and their families: in particular their relationships with social service departments, voluntary organisations and other agencies.

1. Children's rights

Why does equality matter to children? Anyone who has heard the cry 'It's not fair!' or 'But why can't I?' will know part of the answer! Age is a great discriminator, and children are dependent on the goodwill of the adults surrounding them for the achievement of healthy growth and development. We'll be looking in Chapter 4 at how the rights of children and young people being "looked after" (see page for definition) have been affected by the Act and whether the quality of their lives might be improved.

2. Children with disabilities

There are about 360,000 children with disabilities in England and Wales (9). For the first time they will be brought clearly within the remit of local authority child care services, including all the resources, reviews, liaision and planning which that implies. Some of these children will have learned very early about inequalities; but they may not have appreciated the full effect of discrimination on the material, emotional and physical lives of themselves and their family members. Child care specialists new to this area must quickly understand the complex nature of the prejudice that the children and their families can suffer. There may be a need to re-evaluate assessment techniques generally in order that they are appropriate for these children. (See Chapter 3)

3. Children and poverty

In 1987, 20% of all children in Britain were living in families which existed on under half of the average income. This compares to 14% in 1981. (10) The vast majority of children who come into care are from families which rely solely on State benefits. (11)

Many young people leaving home or care have no benefit entitlement until the age of 18 and many are homeless. (12) Children with disabilities live in poorer than average households. (13) Many thousands of low paid workers, the majority of whom are women, exist on little more than those who receive benefit. An increasing number of families have been made homeless as a result of mortgage default and repossessions.

Social work with children is about poverty, of the kind which never goes away and which most of us, as service providers, will never have to experience, and hence will never fully appreciate. The Children Act is coming into force at a time when repressive social security laws have significantly widened the gap between the poorest in the country and the rest of the population. The role of social service departments in the lives of children and their families has become increasingly one of intervention in crisis situations, rather than one of promoting healthy family and community life. There is no avoiding the connections between income maintenance and social work, however, and the Act contains changes which make these clearer than ever, notably:

* the ability to charge families for a wider range of services; many authorities are likely to try and raise income by levying such charges, or will contract out to private concerns who will do so;

* the corporate responsibilities which lay clear duties on different departments; for instance the increased

5

powers to assist certain 16-21 year olds, read together with the duty laid on housing and education departments to co-operate, have financial implications across an authority;

* the duties with major resource implications; there are many, including increased day care provision, duties to consult, to set up new representation procedures, to publicise services and publish reviews and the widening of the definition and circumstances in which an authority can provide cash help for families.

4. Children and racism

Racism which denies black people employment, decent housing and other essentials results in large numbers of black children being amongst some of the poorest children in the country. (14) Research has shown disproportionate numbers of black people living in sub-standard and over crowded accommodation and to be suffering from ill-health. (15) This has been proved to be the direct result of the active racism at work in our public and private institutions. Adult members of black families will all have had to "deal with" racism, and it is a lesson which their children must learn.

Many have developed great strengths in the face of this adversity, and consequently teaching their children the skills for surviving and feeling proud in a white, racist society. Some families must, for example, continue to live in neighbourhoods where a relative or friend has been murdered. Many live in fear of arson and bomb attacks; black women will have been subjected to sexist and racist abuse on the streets; and all will have suffered at the very least by the sight of racist graffiti. Racist attacks are both personal and impersonal; personal in the sense that an individual's body, self-esteem and emotions are under attack, and impersonal in the sense that the individual is not seen at all - only the skin colour is relevant to the attacker. To convey such horrors to children in order to prepare them to defend

themselves and to grow into integrated, positive adults is a major task of all black adults. It also becomes the responsibility of all social workers and carers who work with black children and their families.

The Children Act is unique in child care legislation because it takes into account, for the first time, the multi-ethnic and multi-cultural nature of our society. It implies by this inclusion that there is something significant about these factors which affect the way in which problems should be assessed, policies written and services delivered. The implication extends to all social workers in all situations in order that:

* they are actively aware of the cultural and ethnic origins of themselves and their clients;

* they are doing their best to work against racism at all times;

* their actions recognise, value and build on the strengths and achievements of black children, rather than engaging in overt or covert attacks on them.

The Children Act does not represent equal opportunities legislation. It is, however, supported by the Race Relations Act 1976 which already enables policy makers to take steps to fight against the unequal provision of services to black and minority ethnic members of society.*

*FOOTNOTE: It is important to remember that it is still possible to make positive use of this legislation even though people will have moved on over the years in their use of language and understanding of racism.

III. FOCUS ON DISABILITY

A brief glance at the past 50 years of legislative duties and voluntary effort in the field of disability shows a lack of inter-departmental cohesion and accountability which may be unequalled in all our health, education and welfare services. Before we unravel some of those issues, it may be helpful to be reminded of some of the more familiar laws.

The history of service provision

1948

National Assistance Act: contains the definition of "disabled" which is echoed in the Children Act. The 1948 Act says: "Persons who are blind, deaf or dumb, or who suffer from mental disorder of any description, and other persons who are substantially and permanently handicapped by illness, injury or congenital deformity" (s.29) Local authorities were given responsibility for non-specialist provision.

1970

Chronically Sick and Disabled Persons Act: local authorities were recommended to improve services to disabled people.

1970

Local Authorities Social Services Act:the Seebohm reorganisation of specialist services into unified departments.

1970

Education (Handicapped Children) Act: education services for mentally handicapped children transferred from health to local authorities.

1970

Attendance Allowance introduced.

1975

Mobility Allowance and other benefits introduced.

1979

Warnock Report: recommended greater integration of children with special needs into mainstream schools.

1981

Education Act : wider choice to parents of special needs children; the process of "statementing".

1986

Disabled Persons (Services, Consultation and Representation) Act: disabled people and their representatives can require local authorities to assess their needs.

1986

Social Security Act: revision of the benefit system.

1988

Supplementary benefit replaced by income support and social fund.

Chapter 1

*Social Work &
the History of
Discrimination*

What are some of the problems associated with this lack of an overall strategy?

i) a lack of relevant information made available to both family members and professionals, partly due to problems of definition of disability; for example a reliance on disease categorisation rather than effect on daily life;

ii) a lack of corporate planning of services, as a result, with no mutually agreed methods of recording and sharing vital information between departments and agencies;

iii) differences of approach which have hampered good quality care; for example, by taking a narrow medical approach to rehabilitation which doesn't take account of the socio-economic needs of children with disabilities and their families;

iv) an over-reliance by service providers on the informal care network, which overburdens women in particular and causes emotional, physical, and material hardship to whole families;

v) failure to consider the particular needs of black and minority ethnic children who have a disability, by focussing on the disability, and ignoring their black identity;

vi) a lack of serious attention to the financial position of families; for example, the significant drop in living standards caused by the introduction of new social security laws, and the failure to recognise the true financial costs of caring for a person with a disability;

vii) very low resource provision, especially in domiciliary services, and particularly as the cost of residential care increased;

viii) failure to consult at all satisfactorily with either the children or their representatives; and

ix) the continued use of offensive language, arising from the lack of co-ordinated change to the various laws applicable to children and adults; this is noticeable in the Children Act (Chapter 3, p. 62 for further discussion).

There are areas in the country, however, where excellent services are sensitively provided and adequately resourced. The problem is that these have developed as a result of pressures from national and local pressure groups or by committed individuals and groups, rather than as a result of national streamlining and upgraded standards, which are supported by the highest level policies and budget commitments. For example, Barnardo's has prioritised children and families affected by AIDS/HIV in its coming year's programme and has established contacts with health authorities; Harlesden Community Mental Handicap Team in the London Borough of Brent re-appraised their work with black and white families in their area after receiving the results of a questionnaire; (16) Lewisham Contact a Family service (a self-help group for children with special needs) employed a black worker and set up separate black support groups. (17)

Policies and resource allocation within local authorities

Since 1970, housing departments have been required to have regard to the special needs of the chronically sick; social service departments have been required to undertake necessary adaptations to property. In addition, authorities were to inform themselves about those with disabilities in their area and advise them of services to which they were entitled. There is no doubt that many authorities took these duties very seriously, but it is also true that these budgets were a target of the hefty cuts being made throughout the next 20 years, as public expenditure diminished. In 1991, many authorities are looking to make even more cuts and the signs for the kind of resource provision needed for those with disabilities are not encouraging.

As well as a lack of money to fund suitable housing and adaptations, residential care and domiciliary services, there is generally a lack of expertise and status in this area of work. Again, there are many professionals whose work is highly regarded and who have built solid foundations for across the board co-operation, for example through the District Handicap Teams (see previous pages). In many social service departments though, work with both children and adults with disabilities is poorly resourced in terms of staff time, salaries and experience. This is despite the fact that, of such children living away from home, 15% do so because of physical or sexual abuse and a further 33% come from "unsuitable homes". (18) This means that at least 48% are in need of skilled and extensive help in relation to their families, their own place within their families, and their emotional, physical and social health as a result of the difficulties they have experienced. If child protection work normally commands the highest priority, what is happening to them and how far do social workers feel equipped through knowledge, skill and experience to help them?

A Department of Health (D.o.H.) -funded review of English local authorities' child care policy documents was conducted in 1990.(19) It noted that reference to children with disabilities was generally absent from policy statements and aims. Discussion of the health and education needs of children in care and their future employment prospects was also missing. These gaps will require urgent attention as documents are revised in the light of the Children Act.

Partnership with families

One obvious source of advice and expertise is the child's family, including those families where abuse has taken place. Most workers in this field would readily acknowledge that the families are the experts - through intimate, daily caring for a child they are alert to the slightest change in health or development, are able to assess what kinds of services are needed and what future needs are likely to be. They will also have become expert at dealing with a bewildering range of professionals and agencies and may know much more about benefit entitlement than most social workers.

There is some evidence to show that the

increase in self-help pressure groups, the growth of advocacy and self-determination in the 1970s, and the general trend towards consumerism during the 1980s have assisted an understanding both of the rights and abilities of those with disabilities to take part in the design of services generally and decisions about their own lives in particular. Virginia Beardshaw notes this trend in both the Griffiths Report, "Community care: agenda for action" and the Wagner Report, "Residential care: a positive choice". She comments:

"The approach to accommodation and social support outlined in the two reports is one that could offer a constructive way forward for people with physical disabilities. In particular, it offers the potential for far greater user participation in service design and delivery, with the possibility of direct user control of services becoming a general option through community care allowances. " (20)

Practice guidelines have been drawn up for those working together with families to harness that expertise and knowledge. Professionals who attempt to make plans without them miss a vital ingredient in the process. (See the guidelines in Chapter 3, page 68)

Families in poverty

Families in which there is a child with a disability, are families in which each person is affected materially, physically, emotionally and socially by that disability. Women, in particular, become unpaid carers of their children and their chances of increased earnings or career development diminish. Depending on the disability, brothers and sisters may have less freedom, less space, less attention, fewer toys, clothes and holidays. It is also certain that all such families will be affected by less money; less time or opportunity to earn it and additional expenditure on essentials such as food, laundry, clothes, transport and adaptations.

The Office of Population, Censuses and Surveys (OPCS) report 1989 showed that whether in work or out, these families were significantly poorer than average house-

Chapter 1

Social Work & the History of Discrimination

Chapter 1

*Social Work &
the History of
Discrimination*

holds, and that children with disabilities can look forward to a future of poverty if the figures continue. It states that 75% of disabled adults in private households relied on State benefit as their main source of income. (21) Any change in social security laws therefore is crucially important to their well being. These are people who have been poorly served in recent years by the change to housing benefit, the attempted introduction of the community charge, reduction of child benefit and the shift from supplementary benefit to income support and the introduction of the Social Fund.

Prior to April 1988, a family on supplementary benefit with a child with disabilities could have claimed specific extra amounts for heating, special diets, heavy laundry costs and domestic assistance. These "extras" were frequently underclaimed but were based on the actual costs of the disability. The replacement in income support is a flat-rate "Disabled Child Premium". It is only paid to those children who are getting attendance allowance or mobility allowance or who are registered blind, thus excluding many others who still have a disability. Following the changes in 1986, the Disability Alliance said:

" The best that can be said for the new social security system is that it has been an appalling failure as far as people with disabilities have been concerned, representing the most savage attack on their living standards". (22)

Interconnection with racism

Two particular issues need to be highlighted here in respect of service delivery to black and minority ethnic children with disabilities:

Access to services

Research conducted in 1987 (23) and 1989 (24) into service delivery by local authorities showed that they were delivered unequally to black and white communities. This was largely due to the poor publicity and information made available and accessible to black and minority ethnic families, and to the lack of connection felt by them to the organisation. It was clear to the authors of one report that low take up of services in that area did not reflect a different level of need between the two communities (white and Asian). They said:

".. discussion of the "special" or "additional " needs of Asians can be highly misleading. This is not so much because such needs do not exist as because such terms imply that something extra is to be granted to the disadvantaged groups from the baseline of parity in service delivery. This is quite likely to offend ethnic minorities who perceive it as a misrepresentation of the true situation and offend whites who perceive it as an intention to (positively) discriminate against them. The risk is that attention to cultural differences should distract attention from the main task of ensuring equality of provision of ordinary services for ordinary needs " (24, p.40).

Assessment of services needed

The task then is to acquire information and assess the situation without falling into the trap of making cultural assumptions, whilst at the same time being alert to the particular external pressures often experienced by black citizens. Recently completed research into the assessment of black and minority ethnic people with learning difficulties (25) found, in testing children that:

" Such tests are based on the assumption that the individuals will identify with images based on white middle class lifestyles and experiences."

The authors found evidence that inappropriate testing has contributed to disproportionate numbers of minority ethnic children being placed in special schools. They highlight several initiatives around the country which are gradually moving towards greater involvement of children and parents in the assessment, and thereby arrive at more accurate and satisfactory conclusions.

The experiences of children with disabilities and their families, some of which we have highlighted here, show that the support they receive from national and local government is extremely variable, both in availability and quality. These children, more than their able-bodied counterparts, require services which have been developed from a high level of inter-departmental and inter-agency co-operation. Their parents and carers, in their turn, require a level of understanding about the particular demands placed on them, which will lead to appropriate service provision. Those families living with the stress of poverty, isolation, racism, housing problems or other difficulties need workers who can make the connections between these and understand the way in which they compound each other.

The challenge to practitioners working with the Children Act, along with other relevant legislation, will be to develop these skills, learning from families and each other.

Assessment work with children with disabilities is discussed in Chapter 3, p. 62

Chapter 1

*Social Work &
the History of
Discrimination*

IV. FOCUS ON RACE

Racism in the provision of social work services to children.

In the glossary on page VI we have defined racism as *"A belief that black people are inferior to white people in relation to their culture, religion, intellect, beliefs, lifestyles."*

Racism manifests itself in a number of ways in social work and social care. In this section, we explore several examples in order to be clear about the context in which the Children Act comes into being.

Denying black people access to services.

The failure of departments to respond adequately to the needs and interests of black communities has been thoroughly documented.

In 1978, the Association of Directors of Social Services (ADSS) said:
"Our conclusion is that the response of social service departments to the existence of multi-racial communities has been patchy, piecemeal and lacking in strategy." (26)

In 1982, the British Association of Social Workers (BASW) said:
" And it is no longer adequate to shelter behind alibis of lack of resources to implement change when the true obstacle is lack of will. " (27)

In 1987, the Social Services Inspectorate (SSI) said:
"If discrimination on the grounds of need is the norm in the provision of personal social sevices, then the evidence...indicates that Afro-Caribbean and Asian clients are experiencing an abnormal service. " (28)

In 1988, the SSI positively stated:"
The Inspectorate is committed to promoting the delivery of accessible and cost-effective personal social services which are appropriate to the needs of a multi-racial and multi-cultural society giving full regard to the different needs and expectations of people from a variety of races and cultures." (29)
The SSI 1987 report noted that there had been slight improvements during the early 1980s which they attributed to a combina-

tion of responsiveness to inner city disorder, an exploitation of new funding opportunities and pressure from black staff, black elected members and black communities. Such gains, however, cannot be consolidated and sustained without a corporate decision within the local authority to actively oppose racism, together with financial and policy back-up.

Ignoring black clients and workers

The fashion to integrate black clients into a white system by insisting that services and practice should be good enough for all has been a common and misguided attempt to avoid grasping the points made in the reports outlined above. It has resulted in further years of racist working practices. In 1984, the Black and in Care Conference said:
"For most of these young people, the care experience had been one in which their colour was at best ignored." (30)

In 1985, the SSI, in an inspection report, found that more than half of the 149 homes inspected contained children of non-European origin. The Inspectorate identified *"race relations and the needs of children from ethnic minorities"* as one of the most frequently voiced or observed but unmet needs for training. (31)

In general, institutional racism works to exclude black workers and black citizens through:

*   a lack of ideology which includes black people in determining the strategies and structures which will

go towards meeting their communities' needs;

* a tendency to blanket together all black people and minority ethnic groups so that there is talk of "the black community" as if it were homogeneous;

* no built- in systems which provide a direct route from black citizens to the organisation at power level;

* neutralising black staff by marginalising them to special interest posts, combined with an inability to see their skills and knowledge in a wider context;

* no political education of union members or leaders and no support from national parties; and

* a fear of loss of power by senior managers and others which pervades the system.
(32)

Basing assessments on prejudice and negative beliefs

There are numerous examples of this behaviour in social work, many from the field of mental health work. A typical way in which it can operate is outlined on page 69 (research re: .black children with learning difficulties)

At a conference in 1990 (33), Bandana Ahmad, director of the Race Equality Unit at the National Institute of Social Work, noted that social work operates within a deficit or dysfunctional theory of family life; when this is applied to black families it is even more damaging because it is compounded by racist generalisations, racist assumptions and ignorance. (see Chapter 3 for further discussion)

Discriminatory intervention

Again, examples are growing to show that black families are being discriminated against by society's most powerful justice and welfare institutions.

During the debate on the Criminal Justice Bill in December 1990, there were calls for amendments to force criminal courts to avoid racial discrimination in sentencing. *"Ethnic minorities constituted only about 5 per cent of the British population. But, according to official figures, about 16 per cent of the prison population came from ethnic minorities last year...Black and Asian women accounted for 24 per cent of the female prison population...black people on entering prison had on average fewer convictions than white prisoners."* (The Independent 7/12/90)

There has been much concern, over the past 20 years, despite difficulties in collecting and analysing data, about the growing numbers of black children in care. Reasons for this are statistically difficult to evaluate. Cheetham (34) suggests that the theory that the situation simply reflects the disproportionate degrees of poverty and deprivation which black people face, may not be the case; she notes that black parents had fewer relatives to turn to in crisis, and that there were considerable misunderstandings between them and social workers about the nature of their difficulties.

Failure to monitor or evaluate policies and services

In 1978, the Association of Directors of Social Services (ADSS) recommended that there was an urgent need to review all work; that the major part of the review should be local; that it was crucial to include minority ethnic communities; that monitoring of staff and consumers was essential and that additional resources from central government were required to enable the review. (35) Shama Ahmed, in commending ethnic monitoring to social service departments, makes the straightforward case that reliable data replaces guesswork. (36)

Chapter 1

*Social Work &
the History of
Discrimination*

We live in a society where people are damaged every day by irrational and unfair prejudice, where most of us have been raised and have absorbed this prejudice at every level of our understanding and where most of our institutions continue to promote some kind of prejudice in their service delivery. Many such examples can be found in schools: the assembly arrangements and holiday system are usually arranged around Christian festivals so that children of other faiths become different and have to make special arrangements. Social workers are conditioned, along with everybody else, by our schools and colleges, by "public opinion" and by our perceived experience, to the nature and acceptability of prejudice.

Social work education

Social work education, it seems, has not risen to the challenge this poses. Recently a group of black students on a Certificate of Qualification in Social Work course gave voice in the social work press to their dismay and anger that their teachers and white co-students had failed so completely to include an adequate, informed view about working with black families in Britain.

Student textbooks, teaching methods and underlying philosophies still largely promote Eurocentric *(see glossary)* attitudes to social work, still fail to challenge assumptions about family life, about sexual identity *(see glossary)* and about the "normality" of the able-bodied. In addition, such attitudes actually reinforce negative perceptions of many people because they fail to inform about the diversity and strength of the many religions, languages, cultures and ethnic communities which enrich and change British society. (37) Essentially, we are not equipped by our training to fully understand the ways in which our society in general, our own agencies, in particular, and we as workers continue to oppress many people in the community - most especially our clients. The Central Council for Education and Training in Social Work (CCETSW) has recently responded by publishing a series of books on anti-racist knowledge and practice. (38)

The purpose of social work

Social work as a profession is at the cutting edge of discrimination. Our work is rooted in the pain and suffering of people who are struggling against odds which are sometimes too great, whether that is due to illness, poverty, racism, homelessness or other strains and pressures. It is sometimes so obvious that we forget it is there. We become inured to the chronic misery and debilitating effects of poverty, to the degradation and hopelessness of living in "temporary accommodation", to the frustration of being unable to communicate through language or disability problems. We ignore it because it is too awful even to experience second-hand, or it is too close to our own lives to be bearable. A few ignore it because they really are too removed from the daily effects of injustice to understand its damaging effects.

Whatever our personal history and understanding, we are in a profession which charges us with a responsibility to deal - one way or another - with inequalities and injustice, with getting people a fair deal, with helping people to make themselves safe and healthy. Depending on our position within organisations, we may think that our contribution is a modest one, or that the task is overwhelming. Both of these may be true, but what will matter will be a commitment to opposing the discrimination which injures clients and ourselves.

The Children Act and discrimination

The "spirit" of the Act has already begun to be discussed at some length. People are aware of the big gap between minimal implementation and being true to what is regarded as the meaning and intention behind it. Much of this philosophy is given a sense of reality in the Principles and Practice guide.

The Act's main principles can be summarised as follows:

1.
Children are generally best cared for within their own families, and local authorities have duties to support this.

2.
The courts' duty, in considering any matter before it, is to make the welfare of the child its paramount concern.

3.
The State should not intervene in family life unless there are clear reasons for doing so, and court orders should not be granted unless they can be shown to be of positive benefit.

4.
Private and public law are integrated so that the courts' duties apply in all situations.

5.
Local authorities are to work in partnership with families, who retain parental responsibility for their children.

6.
Local authorities, when making certain decisions about children, must have regard to their racial origin, cultural and linguistic background and religious persuasion.

7.
The courts have wider powers to use directions and private law orders in care proceedings in order to make flexible and specific provisions.

There is no doubt that the Act's intention is that professionals work much more in partnership with families and colleagues from other agencies. That means participation and power sharing. Obvious examples of this are found in the new ability of parents and others with parental responsibility to remove their child from accommodation without notice; in the courts' power to ask social workers what their plans are for a child if a care order were to be made; in the establishment of representations and complaints procedures which a wide range of people can use. Local authorities are encouraged to devolve some of their service provision to others, particularly voluntary organisations, and are to undertake new duties, such as the review of day care, in conjunction with the education authority.

For some workers, this will involve a considerable change in their relationships with their clients and community and their employer and colleagues from other disciplines. Participation, whether in direct work or in decision-making at policy level, presupposes a close relationship between client and worker; not necessarily one of agreement or even of mutual liking, but one which acknowledges that each person has a responsibility and a role to play, without which a problem cannot be resolved. It is at this point that the power imbalance between client and worker is at its most acute; one person has the problem after all, and the other has the power to enforce a particular course of action. Working in this way is difficult and challenging, and because of this, many workers choose, consciously or not, a less demanding and ultimately less threatening way of dealing with clients. For example, many reasons are found not to invite family members to case conferences; many local authorities do not routinely give families information when a child is admitted to care, or they make that information in some way inaccessible; very few ask community groups for advice about policy making and resource allocation.

Social workers and their managers, on training courses and in reading about the Chil-

Chapter

Social Work & the History of Discrimination

Chapter 1

Social Work & the History of Discrimination

dren Act, will no doubt be checking to see what's familiar and what's different from current laws and practice. Everyone needs this sense of comparison to assess the extent of change required by themselves and their colleagues. However, the temptation then is to look at existing policies and procedures and see how they can be adapted to suit new requirements; essentially what is the minimum necessary in terms of understanding, effort and resource allocation to accommodate this new law. In some situations, this will lead to a continuation of existing discriminatory policies and practice. Another, more challenging and exciting way to read and understand the Act is to search for the specific ways in which it can support positive practice on issues of equality, and we hope that this guide helps with that.

What we cannot help with, though, are the pressures to which all practitioners are increasingly susceptible and which necessarily take their toll on good practice. Working in a context of direct cuts of services and jobs; of departmental re-organisation; of hostile media attacks and public opinion; and of increasingly difficult caseloads inevitably results in tired, angry and depressed staff, and more people leaving the profession altogether. It is hard to initiate and sustain high principles and standards in these circumstances. What we hope is that readers will find some encouragement and some new ideas to try out with colleagues which will mean taking practical steps to a better social work service.

IDEAS FOR ACTION

What can you do?

As a starting point, you can:

1. Be aware

Be aware of the power you have by virtue of the position you hold within a large and powerful organisation, in relation to your clients: power to give and withhold services, to remove the liberty of some clients, to protect vulnerable people from getting hurt, to profoundly influence the lives of children you are looking after.

2. Discuss

Discuss with your team/ supervisor ways in which it would be positive and appropriate for you to share some of that power with others; for example, by asking for advice from someone new, by changing your routine about how decision-making meetings are held, by involving clients in producing new publicity information.

3. Be open

Be open to the idea that there are perspectives apart from your own, some of which may be right!

4. Be ready

Be ready to challenge your own and other agencies' discriminatory policies. You can write to the director or assistant director, or get your team to send a letter together; tell your shop steward and ask for the union to take action; re-write the policy yourself and send your ideas to others for comments; inform your clients if you think the agency is acting illegally or discriminating against them and help them find an advocate.

5. Be prepared

Be prepared to give your clients access to advisors and agencies that can give them independent advice, and may oppose you; such as local solicitors, Child Poverty Action Group, Children's Legal Centre, Family Rights Group and local law centres.

Finally - *have some fun!*

Find something you think you will enjoy doing with a client or a colleague and agree with your supervisor that it gets included in your work schedule:

- *yes*, it's important
- *yes*, there's time
- *yes*, because if you don't, you'll give up!

Part of the challenge in finding new ways of working within the framework of the Children Act will be to learn new methods which are not only effective and pay sufficient respect to people, but which include people in ways that build on their strengths and abilities. This includes you, your strengths and your abilities.

Chapter 1

Social Work & the History of Discrimination

CHAPTER 1
REFERENCES

1. **Households below average income:** a statistical analysis 1981-1987 DHSS May 1988

2. **Child poverty and deprivation in the U.K.** J.Bradshaw, National Children's Bureau (NCB) 1990

3. **The exclusive society: citizenship and the poor** R.Lister, Child Poverty Action Group (CPAG) 1990

4. **Joseph Jackson Memorial Lecture 1989** New Law Journal 14/4/89 p.508

5. **Social Trends 20** HMSO 1990

6. **Families in the future** Study Commission on the Family 1983

7. as above no.6 p.19

8. **Social Trends 20**

9. **Surveys of disability in Great Britain no.3 1989** Office of Population, Censuses and Surveys (OPCS)

10. as above no.1

11. **Poor clients:** the extent and nature of financial poverty amongst consumers of social work services (of 73,000 referrals 1984-5, 88% had welfare benefit as major source of income) S. Becker and S. McPherson, Notts. University Benefits Research Unit 1986

12. **Young Runaways** (34% of 532 run-aways were from local authority care; cf. in care group less than 1% of total child population) C. Newman, Children's Society Central London Teenage Project 1989

13. **Surveys of disability in Great Britain no. 5 1989** OPCS

14. **Black and white Britain. 3rd Policy Studies Institute study.** C. Brown, Heinemann 1984

15. **Social work, racism and black communities: a bibliography** N. Ahmad, Race Equality Unit (REU) National Institute for Social Work (NISW) 1990

16. **Double Discrimination: issues and services for people with learning difficulties from the black and ethnic minority communities** p.189 C. Baxter, K.Poonia, L.Ward, Z. Nadirshaw, King's Fund/ Commission for Racial Equality (CRE) 1990

17. as above no.16, p.191

18. **Surveys of disability in Great Britain no. 2 1989** OPCS

19. **Child care policy: putting it in writing. A review of English authorities'child care policy statements** D.Robbins, Social Services Inspectorate(SSI), HMSO 1990

20. **Last on the list: community service for people with physical disabilities** Virginia Beardshaw, King's Fund Institute 1988

21. as above, no.18

22. **Disability Rights Handbook no.14** The Disability Alliance Era 1990

23. **Race, community groups and service delivery** H.Jackson and S. Field, Home Office research and planning unit 1989

24. **Disability and ethnic minority communities** - a study in 3 London boroughs
A.Nathwani and N.Perkins, Greater London Association for Disabled People 1987

25. as above, no.16

26. **Multi-racial Britain : the social services response** p.14
Association of Directors of Social Services (ADSS)/ CRE 1978

27. **Social work in multi-cultural Britain**
British Association of Social Workers (BASW) 1982

28. **Race and culture in social services delivery: a study in 3 social service departments in NW England** p.6
R. Hughes and R.Bhaduri, SSI 1987

29. **Social services in a multi-racial society,** p.23
R.M.Pearson, SSI 1988

30. **Black and in care conference report**
Children's Legal Centre 1985

31. **Inspection of community homes**
SSI 1985

32. **Translating race equality policies into practice**
A. Gurnah, Critical Social Policy Issue 27, 1989/90

33. **Working with the strengths of black families: study day report**
REU, NISW/London Boroughs Training Committee (LBTC) 1990

34. **Social work with black children and their families**
eds. S. Ahmed, J.Cheetham, J.Small, Batsford 1985

35. as above, no.26

36. **Race and social work: a guide to training**
eds. V.Coombes and A.Little, Tavistock 1986

37. **Anti-racist social work: a challenge for white practitioners and educators**
L.Dominelli, Macmillan 1988

38. **Anti-racist social work education**
CCETSW 1991

FURTHER READING SUGGESTIONS

1. **Poverty and anti-poverty strategy: the local government response**
S. Balloch and B.Jones, Association of Metropolitan Authorities 1990

2. **Women, the family and social work**
eds. E. Brook and A. Davis, Tavistock 1985

3. **Feminist social work**
L.Dominelli and E.McLeod, Macmillan 1989

4. **Women and social work**
J.Hanmer and D.Statham, Macmillan 1988

5. **Out of the doll's house**
A.Holdsworth, B.B.C. 1988

6. **Sister outsider**
A.Lorde, Crossing Press Feminist Series 1984

7. **Section 28: law, myth and paradox**
D.Evans in Critical Social Policy Issue 27, Winter 89/90

8. **Lesbian families: cultural and clinical issues**
M.Hall in Social Work USA Vol.23 no. 5 Sept. 1978

9. **The unequal challenge: bringing race and culture into the mainstream of social services provision**
J.Kwhali and T.Mukherjee, Focus Consultancy Ltd./Local Government Management Board forthcoming

10. **The politics of disablement**
M.Oliver, Macmillan1991

CHAPTER 2
SOCIAL WORK AGENCIES AND THE COMMUNITY

PRINCIPLES OF THE ACT		
Children are best looked after within their own families.	State intervention should be kept to a minimum.	When local authorities are looking after children, they should try to place them with or near family and friends and promote contact between them.

DUTIES AND POWERS		
Identify extent of children in need in the area. Sch.2(1)	Open and maintain a register of disabled children. Sch.2(2)	Provide services to children in need and their families in the community. Part III & Sch.2
Prevent children suffering ill-treatment or neglect. Sch.2(4)	Have regard to the racial origin of children in need when encouraging foster care applications and arranging day care. Sch.2(11)	Publish information about services available under Part III Sch.2(1)

PRINCIPLES AND PRACTICE GUIDE			
No.2	**No.3**	**No.21**	**No.34**
Although some basic needs are universal, there are a variety of ways of meeting them.	Children are entitled to protection from neglect, abuse and exploitation.	Since discrimination of all kinds is an everyday reality in many children's lives, every effort must be made to ensure that agency services and practice do not reflect or reinforce it.	When alternatives are being considered and/or decisions made, certain individuals or groups may need to be involved.

EQUALITY ISSUES			
Developing knowledge of the community, including its history, ethnicity, household composition, employment and income patterns.	Recognising the importance of, and connections between, different forms of discrimination.	Understanding the power of the social work agency and being prepared to share that power with the community, by e.g. promoting client participation in service development.	Producing publicity which is relevant and accessible to everyone in the area, encouraging equal access to services.

CHAPTER 2
SOCIAL WORK AGENCIES AND THE COMMUNITY

I.   CONSULTATION OR PARTICIPATION?

The principle of working in partnership is explicit in a number of the new duties and powers in the Children Act; it is implicit in many others, and there has been considerable publicity given by the Department of Health to the importance of taking it seriously. (For example, in the Guidance and Regulations Volume II) Later in this guide there will be some discussion about how this might work in individual relationships between social worker and client. (For example, children and young people as partners, Chapter 4)

The local authority has legal duties, and other agencies are legally constituted to carry out specific functions. How do these organisations work as partners with the communities they serve, and with each other, and how does this affect equal access to their services and equal care and attention for all children and their families?

Working with your community

Most social work agencies would probably say that they believe they work in some kind of partnership with their local community, and new laws are encouraging this development; for example in access to files legislation and in requiring the establishment of representations and complaints procedures. There are many examples - holding public meetings over plans to build a new hostel for people with learning difficulties; allocating funds for self running centres; having regular input to race and disability committees. The perspective of people who use those services or are affected by the powers of the organisation is likely to be very different, and the reasons for this discrepancy are highlighted by Suzy Croft and Peter Beresford in their research into increasing user participation in social services.(1)

The essential difference, they say, is that any attempt at user involvement by the organisation is service provider - led; its aims are therefore likely to be to meet the aims of the agency in one way or another. On the other hand, any attempt at involvement which is service user - led will attempt to meet their needs. These basic starting points have led many individuals, groups and organisations into conflict, often because their initial intentions have been unclear and misunderstood.

Local authorities which decide not to consult the public about the Act's definition of "in need" and their own criteria for service provision run the risk of setting up inappropriate services and perpetuating a mistrustful relationship between service providers and users.

" We want to run the services along with those who do so now. They don't think we are capable. If only they came to our meetings they would understand and learn a lot from us".
(Members of a self-advocacy organisation of people with learning difficulties). (2)

Parents have a view too

SIR — We are a group of parents of troubled teenage boys, who have been meeting regularly over the last eight weeks. Some of our discussions have centred on our feelings about the involvement of professionals in our lives.

As a result of these we have come up with ten rules which we would like them to bear in mind when dealing with parents in our position:

1. Try to keep appointments and be on time. If you have to cancel, try to let us know — remember, we will be sitting and waiting.

2. Remember we have feelings. We try to trust you, so think how we feel when you announce you will no longer be visiting us or are handing us over to someone else with very little warning.

3. Many of us are on very limited incomes. We need the money up front for visits, etc, rather than be paid afterwards. We also resent spending a fortune trying to track you down on the phone.

4. If you get things wrong, just say sorry, do not fob us off with excuses.

5. Treat us as partners: we are concerned about our children and have valuable opinions. Do not put us on trial and make us feel inferior.

6. Could the various professionals consult, so we are not confused by conflicting advice.?

7. Do not forget we have other demands made on us. Remember there is a whole family affected by a son's behaviour.

8. Try and be flexible. A lot of your ideas are all right in theory, but think about the problems of putting them into practice.

9. Tell us if you are going to contact other professionals — do not do it behind our back.

10. Try to explain things clearly, making sure they are understood: both the short and long term consequences.

Division One, Parents Group
Sheffield Metropolitan District Family and Community Services Department.

(source Insight magazine 16/8/90)

Croft and Beresford discuss the results of initiatives on greater user participation currently taking place around the country, and have compiled a list of 12 components which they believe are key to successful outcomes:

*   building in user involvement

*   crucial ingredients - support and access

*   involving minority ethnic groups

*   user involvement when rights are at risk giving people information, skills and support

*   the economy of involvement - it can save time and money

*   consumerism versus self-advocacy - the importance of distinguishing between them

*   the emergence of self-advocacy

*   having an agency strategy for involvement

*   lack of information -it leads to confusion

*   collective action can be effective

*   involving the workers

*   guidelines from experience

They include useful tips for getting started with new initiatives, and how to avoid the kind of difficulties which others have experienced.

> **FACT BITE:**
>
> 1987: 'the total weekly income of one-parent families equalled 36.7% that of two-parent families. (3)
>
> **FACT BITE:**
>
> 1985: 'of 73,000 referrals to a social services department, 88% had a welfare benefit as their major source of income.(4)

The challenge to local authorities will be how to respond positively to the logic of this situation without falling into the trap of stigmatising, labelling and blaming whole sections of society, and regarding them primarily as "problem families."

There is no doubt also that the unfortunate use of the term "in need", which conjures up visions of destitute and hungry children, will in itself be sufficiently off-putting to prevent some families from telling social workers or others of their difficulties. To be labelled in this way in order to receive a service will work against the Government's intention of making such services more "user-friendly," informal and participative. If it can be assumed that all children have needs which can only be met with adult assistance and that some simply need more help than others, then both staff and service users will require information from managers which reflects this belief and enables them to work together.

Black families are already well aware of these problems; much has been written about the appalling failure of social work to understand their strengths and abilities and therefore to accurately assess their needs. (5) The principle of working in partnership, together with new duties to find out about local levels of need, present managers and practitioners with an excellent opportunity to set in motion a more positive approach. Departments could ask the advice of local black and minority ethnic groups and individuals involved in child care services regarding how they define the extent of need in relation to themselves, families and friends; how racial origin can most helpfully be recorded; and how the authority can then begin to establish " a range and level of services which are appropriate to those children's needs".

CHECKPOINT:

Does your agency encourage either consultation with, or the participation of, children, their families or representatives in your area? If so:

* who decides which groups or individuals are consulted?

* what is the purpose of any such process?

* do the people consulted agree that it is useful?

* how do you resolve conflicts?

* what independent elements are built into the process?

Working with local agencies

In addition to public consultation, the Act also gives local authorities new duties and powers to work together with other authorities, agencies and individuals. For example:

"Every local authority shall facilitate the provision by others (including in particular voluntary organisations) of services which the authority have power to provide by virtue of this section or section 18, 20, 23 or 24..." s.17(5)

The spirit in which this kind of work is established and sustained will make a substantial difference to the lives of children and families. It is already the case that some authorities have withdrawn funding from voluntary groups in their areas, effectively closing them down altogether. The s.17 duty poses the question whether local authorities will simply interpret this as permission to contract out any of their services, from day care to home helps and foster care, or whether they will use it to encourage the development of those services which they themselves are ill-equipped to provide. Many small groups are completely dependent on local authority funding, and with it provide unique and essential services. These are particularly likely to serve black and minority ethnic families, children with disabilities and women. Being locally based, and often self-running, they are designed to suit consumer need and minimise problems of transport and cost, thereby making them attractive from health, safety and financial perspectives.

There is no doubt that the need to make huge financial cuts will force even more local authorities into considering the closure of such groups, which, it may be argued, meet the needs of only a small minority. The effect of such closures, however, is to further discriminate against members of the public who are :

a) already experiencing racism, sexism, ablism (*see glossary*) or other forms of discrimination;

Chapter 2

Social Work & the Community

b) have fewest routes into the decision-making process; and

c) may be unable to fight effectively against cuts, due to poverty, fear, inexperience in dealing with bureaucracy, lack of information and support, previous unhelpful contact with the authority and either lack of access to sources of alternative funding, or experience of discrimination on the part of the funding body.

CHECKPOINT:

Do you know which small projects have lost their funding in your neighbourhood? Would they qualify for continuing assistance under s.17(5)? What can you do, as a practitioner or manager within a social work agency, to ensure that those members of the public do not lose access to services? What do you think that others, both within and outside your organisation, could do?

Working with other authorities and with individuals

The review of day care:

" A review ... shall be conducted -
(a) together with the appropriate local education authority" s.19(2)

"Where it appears to a local authority that any authority or other person mentioned in subsection (3) could, by taking any specified action, help in the exercise of any of their functions under this Part, they may request the help of that authority or person, specifying the action in question." s.27(1)

One of the crucial issues facing local authorities, in either facilitating the provision of service by others, or undertaking joint work with them, is the extent to which the

philosophies, aims and practice of the agencies are compatible. All professionals working with vulnerable children will have had some experience of this in the assessments and planning they do to protect and support them; some have developed excellent systems and understanding which have served children well, whilst others struggle to find common ground.

In terms of promoting anti-discriminatory practice, local authorities will want to ensure that any good standards they have established will be continued by others. In some circumstances, they will be able to turn to parts of the Act to insist upon it. For example, anti - racist practice in the provision of day care for children in need is strongly encouraged by:

(a) the duty to "safeguard and promote the welfare of children in their area who are in need" s.17(1)

(b) the duty, when making arrangements for day care, to "have regard to the different racial groups to which children within their area who are in need belong" sch.2(11)

(c) the duty, when cancelling day care registration on the grounds that the care provided is seriously inadequate, to consider the needs of the child, when "a local authority shall, in particular, have regard to the child's religious persuasion, racial origin and cultural and linguistic background" s.74(6).

Similar duties do not exist to protect children against, for example, sexism, but if an authority is drawing up criteria which specifies acceptable and unacceptable provision from an anti-racist perspective, it may decide to develop similar anti-sexist criteria to include in any agreement drawn up with a private contractor.

Working with advisory and advocacy groups

Amongst those to whom a social worker might look for advice is a wide spectrum of local and national groups, which exist specifically as user-member or advocates' forums to enable others to make use of their experience and expertise. Most social work agencies have links with a number of such groups. Some have developed formalised advocacy posts as a result, such as the children's rights officer at Leicester social services department and the appointment in Kent of Suzy Brazier from the Who Cares? project at the National Children's Bureau (NCB), to advise on their fostering scheme.

Chapter

*Social Work &
the Community*

II . KNOW YOUR COMMUNITY

There is one essential step which comes before taking a more detailed look at how your agency may deliver services under the Children Act: finding out what constitutes your community.

Most social workers will have a rough idea about who lives on the local estates or in a particular part of the county, but not many practitioners or area team managers will have the kind of detailed demographic information which helps you to plan for the future needs of your local population. When we look at what is currently happening about unequal access to services (p.28), you may decide that your team needs more accurate knowledge about your potential client group.

TEAM EXERCISE

If this task seems too enormous, try it out with a small estate, a village or a few streets first. Find out what information is already available in the organisation and elsewhere.*

I   HISTORY

*   What is the settlement history of your community?
*   Who settled here and when?
*   What have been the major changes in population?
*   Note major events in the history of your community.
*   What are its traditions and values?

II   POPULATION CHARACTERISTICS

*   What is the population breakdown by:
  age, gender, racial groups, one - or - two parent families, the size of the household, class, families in poverty, homeless persons, numbers employed, the mentally ill, families where a member is seriously disabled, lesbian or gay households.
*   How do these factors cross-reference with each other?

III   INCOME/EMPLOYMENT CHARACTERISTICS

*   What are the main sources of employment and levels of unemployment for:
  the total adult population?
  female/male adult population?
  all ethnic groups?

IV   HOUSING CHARACTERISTICS

*   What is the main housing type?
*   What percentage own/privately rent/rent from council?
*   What percentage of different ethnic groups own/ privately rent/rent from council?

* FOOTNOTE Adapted from Community Practice in Ethnic-Sensitive Social Work Practice by W. Devore and E. Schlesinger

* What types of school are available?
* Are the schools aware of the needs of different groups within the community;
  eg:- are bilingual staff available where needed?
  are buildings accessible to people with disabilities?
* How do they develop a cultural awareness?
* Are there black and minority ethnic head teachers and committee members/
  school governors?
* What are the local health resources?
* Are they aware of the different groups within the community? How?
* What are the prevailing formal/informal networks in the community?
* How do people get any of this information?

VI   *SOCIAL SERVICE FACILITIES*

* What local authority social services are available?
* Are they aware of the different groups in the community?

eg.   are bilingual staff available where necessary?
  are buildings accessible to those with disabilities?
  are there minority ethnic managers and elected members?
  is written information made readily available in all relevant languages?
  what services are used by the community outside the area?
  how accessible are private and voluntary organisations?

Some questions for discussion:

1. How far were you able to provide the answers within your team, or from within your agency?

2. Where are the gaps in your knowledge, and who else can help you fill them in?

3. Are there questions you cannot answer, or feel that you cannot ask?
   If so, how else can you inform yourselves?

4. How can you apply this knowledge to your new duties under Part III and Schedule 2 of the Children Act to provide appropriate services and inform people of them?

5. What are the implications for changing your current practice/allocation of resources?

III. ACCESS TO SERVICES

The question for both workers and managers here is: What do I need to know and understand about my area in order to deliver effective services to the whole community under the Children Act?

It makes sense that those who identify least with service deliverers, or feel that they have most to lose, will not voluntarily request help unless they are in extreme need. For example, lesbian mothers will not seek advice on child care problems for fear of losing custody; refugees will not ask for any help that confirms their dependent status and reinforces perceptions of their inability to take responsibility for themselves; women who have suffered domestic violence will not seek help if they think their ex-partner will be contacted, or that their child may be removed because they are at risk; black grandparents worried about a grandchild's safety, will not want to refer their sons and daughters for fear of racism.

There is a long list. Many people are fearful of contact with the social services and many have good reason. They know that services are not equally delivered and that their referral may be regarded as special, abnormal, pathological or at the least needing particular attention. This special attention is sometimes translated, with the best will in the world, into positive action on behalf of a particular client group. Section 11 posts are an example. Brought in by the Local Government Act 1966, they gave the Home Secretary power to make grants to local authorities *"which, in his opinion, have to make special provision in the exercise of any of their functions in consequence of the presence within their area of substantial numbers of immigrants from the Commonwealth, whose language or customs differ from the community."*

What has happened in practice is that many of these workers have been side stepped in the decisio- making process. Their positions have not been made part of the perma-

nent establishment with clear lines of responsibility and accountability. As a result, they are invited rather than expected to be in decision making groups and their power is neutralised. They are often highly valued by many members of the organisation for their knowledge of a particular community group and their skills in dealing with white staff are extensive. However, the failure to provide such specialist knowledge and skill as part of the establishment is the failure to acknowledge that the community represented is not receiving an appropriate, standard service which is not at risk of being eroded any more than the others. Governmental guidelines on the criteria for s.11 funding were reviewed in 1990. The revisions are designed to make applications cash and time limited, linked to specific projects and liable to monitoring of performance targets. They are to clearly identify disadvantages to be addressed. Project money, however, is not to be used for *"the maintenance of religious, cultural and linguistic traditions amongst ethnic minority communities."* (6)

TEAM EXERCISE

Having identified who lives in your community, (See exercise on p26), how easy is it for different people to approach your office for the same service, e.g. day care for a three year old?

Is the possibility of requesting this service equally accessible to the following :-

1. A 19 year old single black woman, unemployed, able-bodied, working class.

2. Parents with a visual disability, both working full-time, with a child already in school.

3. Grandparents in their 60s, becoming frail, looking after the child of their mentally ill daughter.

4. Mother and stepfather in their 30s, with 5 other children, white working class, running their own business with a child with developmental problems.

What difference would it make to Nos.2 & 3 if the clients were black or white?

*   How do any of the above know that the service exists?

*   Is there written information, and if so, where?

*   Is the written information translated and distributed to places where people can find it?

*   How do people with visual and hearing difficulties get information and make referrals?

*   Is the office open only during office hours, ie., Monday to Friday 9-5, and is it possible to open in the evening or a Saturday morning instead?

*   How do you let people know what is to happen due to staff shortages?

*   Is the office accessible to people with walking difficulties?

*   Is the reception area friendly and welcoming?

*   Are there posters and leaflets in different languages and with different images?

*   Are there reception staff and duty social workers with disabilities?

*   Are there staff from local black and minority ethnic groups?

IV. PUBLICITY AND INFORMATION

Having obtained information about your local area, about services available and relative access to them, there are new duties under the Children Act to make this information available to those who might need them. The relevant duties are:-

1. "(a)   publish information -

   (i)   about services provided by them under sections 17, 18, 20 and 24; and
   (ii)   where they consider it appropriate, about the provision by others (including, in particular, voluntary organisations) of services which the authority have power to provide under those sections; and

   (b)   take such steps as are reasonably practicable to ensure that those who might benefit from the services receive the information relevant to them." sch. 2(2)

2.   to conduct a review of day-care services and "where a local authority has conducted a review under this section, they shall publish the results of the review." s. 19(6)

3.   "establish a procedure for considering any representations (including any complaint) made to them by -

   (a)   any child who is being looked after by them or who is not being looked after by them but is in need;

   (b)   any parent of his;

   (c)   any person who is not a parent of his but who has parental responsibility for him;

   (d)   any local authority foster parent;

   (e)   such other person as the authority consider has sufficient interest in the child's welfare to warrant his representations being considered by them, about the discharge by the authority of any of their functions under this Part in relation to the child." s. 26(3)

CHECKPOINT

Do you know what information was previously made available to your clients, such as:

*   leaflets for children and parents on admission to "care",

*   explanations about the purpose and powers of child protection and other case conferences,

*   information about foster care services,

*   other information, such as when various members of staff are available,

*   leaflets about complaints procedures.

There is a new awareness that much more written information should be given to clients, and that this should be provided as a matter of routine even for people who cannot read. People with no reading skills can usually find someone to read to them and written records can be passed on to advisers and friends. We tend to underestimate the problems of remembering what we have been told when under stress, especially when the service provider is very familiar with the resource. In other aspects of our lives, we expect to get, and very often do, written receipts, guarantees, leaflets, reports, demands and bills. They are one way of measuring the importance of a transaction or fixing an appointment in our memories, of feeling respected and valued, of being able to review and reassess, of referring back to a decision. It is extraordinary that in the field of highly significant work with children and families, which in the worst situation may result in the long term separation of family members against their will, that so little is written down.

When explaining to people what is going on, we also need to remember to explain things more than once. It is easy to forget or misunderstand when you are frightened or angry, and having a friend along can often help.

PERSONAL EXERCISE

If you, your child or someone close to you were involved in the following, what kind of information would you expect to give and receive?

*   The offer of a residential holiday away from the family

*   The provision of a home carer

*   The offer of personal counselling

*   The tenancy of a bedsit

*   A place at a family centre

These kinds of services are to be provided under Part III of the Children Act. If offered on a private basis, you would expect information regarding the trustworthiness and qualifications of the helpers, safety guarantees, specific tasks which would be undertaken, the goals and extent of the counselling, rent and tenancy guarantees and so on. You would also want to know how much you have to pay. Under the Children Act, local authorities can now charge for all services provided under Part III, with one or two exceptions such as counselling and therapy (except to those receiving income support or family credit).

MORE INFORMATION IDEAS

1. 101 Questions and Answers - a revised version forthcoming from Parents Aid Harlow and Family Rights Group.

2. Child Protection Procedures - a guide for families - a revised version to be available from Family Rights Group in English, Hindi, Cantonese, Urdu and Punjabi. (Current edition in Bengali from Tower Hamlets SSD; in Welsh from Gwynedd SSD.)

3. Help Starts Here - A guide for parents of children with a disability, from the National Children's Bureau.

4. All area teams, family centres, etc., should have printed cards with their name, address and telephone number including a number for emergencies; opening times should be listed.

5. All social workers should have printed cards as above.

6. All arrangements for meetings, visits and appointments to be written down.

7. The service, i.e. criteria, costs, extent, assessment and delivery to be in writing. There is an understandable fear that if local authorities inform the local communities that such services are available, then demand will be overwhelming. This makes it even more important that staff and the public are aware of the criteria for receipt of a service. If a client meets the criteria, and the resource is unavailable, this removes the conflict from the personal to the political, and enables the social worker to advise the client about further action. Without such clarity, clients will be tempted to say what they think the social worker needs to hear with unforeseen and possibly damaging consequences.

8. The terms and conditions of the service provided. This may be highly specific, and relate to personal goals or behaviour such as a detailed written agreement regarding work to be undertaken at a family centre for 6 months; or it may be procedural, such as completion of forms and payment of fees for after school care of a young child.

9. All information should be in easily understood English and translated into other appropriate languages and Braille. Translations are sometimes expensive and it is sometimes difficult to persuade managers that this is a priority. However, the local authority has a duty under the Act to provide such information to all members of the community where a child may be in need, and failure to do so will discriminate against them to the extent that they may be denied the provision. Voluntary groups and minority ethnic groups in your area will have experience of the production of such material and may be willing to give advice.

10. Written information should be available to everyone, even if they cannot read. Everyone knows someone who can read a letter to them and it is a continuing mark of your respect for them that you continue to do this.

V. SETTING UP A REPRESENTATIONS AND COMPLAINTS PROCEDURE

A good representations and complaints procedure may be the best advertisement a social work agency can have. A sign of integrity, self-confidence and flexibility, it should be a signal to all members of the community that the organisation respects and values their views and is prepared to open itself to independent inspection. This process does not, of course, work in many areas of the country, due to a combination of low commitment to the principle, low priority being given to allocating resources and the very low regard in which service users hold such procedures.

Inevitably, it is harder for some members of the public to complain than others and this relates back to those who find it hard to get access to services in the first place. Particularly noticeable are those minority ethnic clients who are already disadvantaged by the paucity of information available in their first languages. Children are rarely likely to have adequate information available to them unless they are in a residential establishment with knowledgeable and open staff or informed older children. Children with disabilities are even less likely to be aware of, and able to use, procedures. Finally, families in poverty, however angry or dissatisfied, may lack the necessary resources to follow through a complaint.

Purpose:

CHECKPOINT

* Do you have a complaints procedure in your agency?

* If so, where is it? Do you have a copy?

* How do your clients know that it exists, and how are they encouraged to use it?

The purpose in forcing local authorities into setting up complaints procedures is to ensure that children and those closest to them are properly consulted and informed about decisions that are being made, so that they don't have to try and get redress through the system of judicial review, which is restrictive in who is allowed to apply, and which is not covered by legal aid.

The new duties have the potential for helping practitioners and managers to develop more positive working partnerships with their clients, and particularly to help those with fewest resources at their disposal to present their views.

This procedure is contained in Part III, and relates to how a local authority carries out its functions.

Who can use it?:

"Every local authority shall establish a procedure for considering any representations (including any complaints) made to them by -

(a) any child who is being looked after by them or who is not being looked after by them but is a child in need;

(b) a parent of his;

(c) any person who is not a parent of his but who has parental responsibility for him;

(d) any local authority foster parent;

(e) such other person as the authority consider has a sufficient interest in the child's welfare to warrant his representations being considered by them, about the discharge by the authority of any of their functions under this Part in relation to the child."

s.26(3)

Independent people have to be included:

"The procedure shall ensure that at least one person who is not a member or officer of the authority takes part in -

(a)   the consideration; and

(b)   any discussions... about the action to be taken..." s.26(4)

What must the authority do?:

"... the authority shall-

(a)   have due regard to the findings...

(b)   ...notify in writing...the person who made the complaint, the child (if of sufficient understanding), other people who the authority thinks are likely to be affected, of the decision and the reasons for taking it." s.26(7)

and:

"Every local authority shall give such publicity to their procedure.... as they consider appropriate." s.26(8)

Current situation:

What was the situation before the Children Act came into force, which prompted such a firm push from the Government on this issue? A number of influences can be noted, which include a greater acceptance generally of people's right to complain and a greater readiness to do so. The pressures, policies and changing perceptions of society during the 1980s prompted a hitherto rather reluctant British public to become more vocal and demanding. In addition, there has been a significant growth in the number of self-help and advocacy groups, for example, in the field of disability. Some organisations have worked hard to establish the rights of clients to complain without penalty and have found it a struggle full of obstacles rooted in prejudice, tradition and fear of change. But social service departments can be no exception to this trend

towards greater accountability to the client, especially in view of the enormously powerful role they have in some people's lives. This is slowly being recognised, for example, with regard to access to files legislation and practice.

The Government itself realised that the inclusion of section 26 was necessary as a result of the very poor procedures which currently exist and the high level of dissatisfaction amongst members of the public and others, such as foster carers, about the difficulties in making a complaint. There have also been a number of unusual situations such as young people in residential establishments earmarked for closure, who have needed a clear and accessible system for making representations about decisions to be made about them.

In June 1990, the D.o.H. published the results of a research project into English local authority child care policy statements.(7) Of 107 authorities, 92 responded to the survey. All 15 who did not respond were from the London region. Research by Robbins into the 92 authorities' complaints procedures found that only 34 had one in operation, while 17 were in preparation. Only 4 authorities appeared to have consulted outside organisations in setting up their procedure. It was unclear how many cases had been heard, which may well have been due to poor monitoring procedures. Publicity was found to be poor with information generally only being available to children on admission to care, but not necessarily to their parents. No mention was made in the research of how far information was given to other relatives or interested adults. There was no information about how far publicity was translated or interpreters made available at hearings, nor about the availability of procedures to children and adults with communication difficulties.

Overall, the picture of current provision for the hearing of complaints was found to be very disappointing. Robbins concluded:
".. for those authorities which express concern about clients' rights in their policies, the absence

of any complaints procedure does suggest a serious gap between intention and action." (p.47)

Some of the reasons for this depressing picture have been discussed by Lynne Berry and Nick Doyle in: "Open to Complaints: guidelines for Social Services Complaints Procedures." (8) They suggest that these include:

* attitudes - complaints and complainants are not taken seriously;

* listening to clients - social workers find it difficult to accept criticism, especially in demanding child care work;

* redressing power imbalance - the responsibility for this lies with the social services departments; clients alone cannot make themselves heard;

* need to distinguish between professionals and their provision, ie. between how you do something and your ability to provide it;

* staff protection - the need to look after staff interests is vital;

* funding - local authorities are unwilling to make this a priority and allocate the necessary resources; neither has central government been willing to assist.

How to set it up

So what are the necessary steps towards establishing a good representations and complaints procedure?

1. Consult with community groups, voluntary and other organisations, with clients, carers and staff at all levels. Make active efforts to contact those who might find it particularly hard to find out about the procedure, or to talk to a senior officer from the department or ask others to obtain their views.

2. Appoint a senior officer to undertake the co-ordination of the procedure.

3. Involve trades unions and professional associations.

4. Discuss funding with elected members and agree a budget.

5. Prepare procedures and publicity in line with the guidance and regulations, with the active involvement of people in the consultation groups.

6. Co-ordinate publicity along with that being prepared on services available under Part III.

7. Arrange staff training at all levels.

8. Arrange training for elected members.

9. Liaise with other agencies to discuss co-ordinating with other procedures, especially where responsibility may be held jointly.

10. Draw up a list of independent persons with the assistance of those in the consultation groups. These people should reflect the composition and interests of the community and it is essential that they are seen as truly independent in order for complainants to have confidence in the whole process. It may not be wise, therefore, to make reciprocal arrangements with workers from another authority, or to approach known local professionals such as doctors or guardians *ad litem*. (for example, L.B. Greenwich has developed a scheme with Voice for the Child in Care; Kent C.C. with NAYPIC; authorities in the north west with Independent Representation for Children in Need; Avon with Barnardos)

11. Involve people from the consultation groups in monitoring how effective the procedure has been, and in deciding what changes should be made as a result in the following areas:

a) departmental policies
b) management procedures
c) organisational priorities
d) professional practice
e) future consultation with the community.

Almost all the points above are covered in the draft guidance issued by the D.o.H.(9) It says that procedures..."*should ensure that the individual child, his parents and others significantly involved with the child have confidence in their ability to make their views known and to influence decisions made about the child's welfare.*" (p.4)

The minimum requirements laid down in the guidance should therefore ensure that local authorities establish a solid basis for the development of such confidence. They are encouraged to make:

"*a well -publicised statement of commitment to the representations procedure*" (p.7)

and to their staff:

"*An unequivocal statement on the scope and benefits of the procedure..*"(p.10)

TEAM EXERCISE

* Decide on a complaint and role play your own procedure. (This need not take very long - maybe an hour and a half altogether. Ask a trainer to help you if you think it will help to be clear about roles, etc.)

* **For discussion:**

I is it user-friendly?

II who are the independent people involved?

III how good would it be for dealing with serious complaints, such as that of sexual or racial abuse of a child by a staff member?

IV are you clear about the difference between complaints, disciplinary and grievance procedures and the connection with child protection procedures?

V what would you want to do to improve your procedure, and how can you make these suggestions to the manager responsible for setting it up?

VI. CHILDREN "IN NEED" – SOME IMPLEMENTATION ISSUES

This section looks in broad terms at how the policy makers and budget balancers in local authorities may assess the extent to which children are in need in their area within the context of the Act's framework. This raises questions of how such an assessment will affect and be affected by the community as a whole; and at how the decisions taken may be translated into policy documents for junior managers and practitioners in social service departments, and for staff in other agencies with whom they share some responsibilities. It will be important for practitioners to understand both how these interpretations and decisions are reached locally, and what implications that process has for their own work and service delivery.

1. The duty

"It shall be the general duty of every local authority ...-

(a)   to safeguard and promote the welfare of children within their area who are in need.." s. 17 (1)

"Every local authority shall take reasonable steps to identify the extent to which there are children in need within their area." sch.2 (1)

2. The guidance

What kind of help do authorities receive from the Department of Health in undertaking this complex task? The guidance (10) states:

" The definition of 'need' in the Act is deliberately wide to reinforce the emphasis on preventive support and services to families. It has three categories: a reasonable standard of health or development; significant impairment of health or development; and disablement. It would not be acceptable for an authority to exclude any of these three - for example, by confining services to children at risk of significant harm which attracts the duty to investigate under section 47." (page 5)

This guidance reinforces the letter sent by the Department to directors of social services in January 1991, following concerns that some departments had already begun to restrict the definition in this way.

The guidance continues:

"Local authorities are not expected to meet every individual need, but they are asked to identify the extent of need and then make decisions on the priorities for service provision in their area in the context of that information and their statutory duties." (page 7)

They are clearly aware that local authorities will exercise a high degree of discretion in how they measure the extent of children in need, target their priority groups and decide on criteria for access to services. There are inherent dangers for those who live in areas where the authority are reactive in their methods of measuring the extent of need, target a very restricted band of children and decide on narrow and inflexible criteria, either for political or for financial reasons, or both. Without national guidelines concerning the minimum amount of service people can expect, there is little recourse in the law for members of the public to complain that the extent of need in their community has been wrongly defined and that the authority has therefore not provided a range and level of appropriate services. In the event of such a complaint, some people will have access to the representations and complaints procedure which must be established (see p33) but the child concerned must first be either being "looked after" (see p.86) or already considered to be a child "in need". This means that this procedure cannot be used to complain that a child has been wrongly assessed as not in need.

3. The task

(i) Information-gathering

An urgent job for senior managers will be to collect information in order that they can make recommendations to their elected members and devise appropriate strategies. A working party report points out that reliance on existing methods of information gathering will have its problems.(11) Briefly, they described these as follows:

(a) central government's annual returns on pre-determined data act as a disincentive for departments to develop information systems which reflect their own managerial needs;

(b) information systems in existence are seen as having been created for outsiders and as being of little benefit to either managers or practitioners;

(c) the dynamics of child care work are not reflected in the central government's demands for information. In addition, daily crisis management, especially in "capped" authorities, absorbs all management energies and resources so that forward planning receives little attention. Secondly, these systems are seen by workers as being the tools of senior managers, and as such are mistrusted and not valued.

The working party recognised that in addition to these difficulties, information in relation to the promotion of children's welfare and the provision of support services is likely to be particularly hard to gather in view of the extent of inter-agency activity. They recommend, however :
"that active consideration be given to developing local databases which record such activities and the varieties of intra and inter-agency involvement".

(ii) Which needs are to be met?

Whilst the development of appropriate systems is essential to the planning of services, it requires a vital first step, which is to ask other agencies, departments, community groups and clients about the level of need in the first place. There is no point in recording everyone's level of activity until there is some clarity and agreement about their aims and objectives.

The likelihood is that the great majority of local authorities will tend towards a minor re-shaping of current provision, rather than attempt any kind of radical change to mark a new relationship of power-sharing with the public. This may well be masked by departmental re-structuring and the issues highlighted here lost in fears about re-deployment and redundancy.

(iii) Factors influencing the assessment of the extent of children in need.

What is affecting your managers as they make these decisions in 1991/1992?

(a) history - the traditions, politics and culture of the authority;

(b) current context - the amount of good will, vision, optimism and energy which is available to translate the spirit of the Act into reality;

(c) resources - in a time of rapidly decreasing finance, senior managers and elected members are locked in battles about the services they most want to maintain;

(d) political pressure - central government curbs and local political demands, along with sudden and unpredictable media attention can result in hasty decision-making;

(e) personal beliefs and prejudices - who are your senior managers? What do they believe in; who do they think they represent; do they have an ideological commitment to which the authority/agency is also tied, and what are the practical implications of that ideology?

WE SUGGEST:

In order to carry out the spirit of the legislation, the aims of any emerging child care policy document must be to include:

*Social Work &
the Community*

* the maximum possible level of participation by clients and their advisers, with specific targets, such as the conversion or adaptation of all buildings for access, clients co-opted onto the council, full attendance at case conferences;

* a clear anti-discriminatory statement forming the base line for all policies and procedures, together with an implementation strategy;

* a commitment to safeguard and promote the welfare of children in need;

* a commitment to promote the upbringing of children in need by their own families wherever possible; both of these commitments coupled with strategies to bring them into reality;

* a recognition of the diversity and richness of different lifestyles which contribute to children's healthy growth and development;

* the monitoring and public review of all policies and services;

* seeking the co-operation of other agencies/departments in fulfilling these aims.

VII. REGISTER OF CHILDREN WITH DISABILITIES

"(1) Every local authority shall open and maintain a register of disabled children within their area.

(2) The register may be kept by means of a computer." sch.2(2)

(See Chapter 3, p62. for Act's definition of disability)

This duty is not entirely new; the Chronically Sick and Disabled Persons Act 1970 contained a similar requirement in section 2, but has not been fully implemented. However, this new duty is absolute and may not be avoided.

Some practical implications

1. What is the register for?

The local authority must be clear for themselves, families and other agencies, about the purpose and nature of the register. If, as seems likely, the intention of the legislation is to assist with the planning of future services for children into adulthood (which is why the definition of disability in s.17(11) is similar to that in the National Assistance Act 1948 and which applies to adults), then it should be possible to acquire the necessary information with adequate and appropriate publicity.

There should be no confusion in people's minds between the purpose of this register and that of the child protection register; nor of any list the authority keep regarding children in need. The Act ascribes no protective function to this register at all. Children with disabilities are automatically considered to be children in need (for the purposes of Part III and Schedule 2) but this does not mean that they are necessarily in need of protection. If they are at risk of harm or neglect, other duties in the Act apply as they do to all children.

2. A voluntary record

Despite the local authority's duty to open and maintain the register, there can be no compulsion on parents or other carers to register a child. Unless parents willingly offer information, it will become a mistrusted and useless bureaucratic machine.

Some people are very frightened about giving information about themselves to any official and may not fully understand, or be fully confident, that such information is not passed on to any other government department.

Others will know that their child is already registered by the health and/or education authorities. Assessment under the Education Act (1981) is tantamount to a register, and local education authorites must maintain their records and annually review. Many children are on some form of child health register, and some areas have introduced parent-held health records, which can encourage positive attitudes to the register itself. A joint register may be the best solution in many areas, and inter-agency collaboration be of direct benefit to families.

3. What kind of information?

The Act requires only that a register be opened and maintained. In order to be a "live" and up-to-date working tool, the following might be considered useful:
name ; address ; date of birth ; disability ; extent and nature of disability at present and current level of functioning; predicted nature, extent and functioning; race, culture, religion and language of child and family ; child and family's current needs in respect of the disability (social worker's and family's views) ; child and family's future needs (social worker's and family's views); other agencies/departments in

contact.

Local authorities could consult their local consumer groups to see what kind of information parents felt would be most helpful, and to encourage them to use the register. As parents would have the right to see what is written about them, they might want to be involved in writing their own entry. These can be done imaginatively, and form part of the work already being undertaken between worker and family. They may, for example, like to make a diary of their child's week, as a means of identifying when and how they need support. Another idea would be to list the services they are currently using and where they think the gaps are.

4. Access to the register

Children, young people and their carers need to be secure in the knowledge that the information collected about them is accurate, that they can see it and have access to it at any time and that they can record any changes in circumstances which affect the need for services. Without such active input on the part of families, authorities may find it difficult to meet their duty to maintain the register.

5. A register, not a gatekeeper.

Following on from the principle of voluntary recording, it must be made clear to both practitioners and families that registering a child's name does not guarantee a provision of services, and that failure to register does not mean services will be denied. Although it will be logical for authorities to register all children with disabilities as and when they came to their attention, the legislation does not permit the register to be a pre-requisite for any kind of service.

It is very important to clearly establish this with families at the outset. Experience from the education services indicates that "statementing" came to be regarded by some families as the route to more appropriate and better quality services for their children. As a result, there are now many more appeals against the refusal to make a statement than were ever anticipated.

6. Joint working definition of "disability"

Local authorities do need to establish a definition of disability which is satisfactory both for themselves and for their colleagues in the health and education services. The importance of this can be easily understood when the wide variety of policies on statementing are examined. Some local education authorities will, for example, not necessarily statement a child with spina bifida; another may only do it in order to get a child access to special education provision which would not otherwise be available. It will not be safe, therefore, to say that all children with statements will go on the register.

7. Publicity.

There is no specific provision within the Act for publicising the existence of the register, but it should be included in the general information an authority provides under sch.2(2). In order that families, professionals, volunteers and advocates fully understand its purpose and procedures, posters and leaflets in plain English, other appropriate languages, Braille and on tapes should be prepared and made available in clinics, schools, libraries, advice centres and so on. Advisers should be available in the department to answer specific queries and there should be multi-lingual workers and/or translators as needed.

8. De-registration.

Local authorities might consider whether this concept should be introduced as a way of being alert to changes in children's health and development. This may become an integral part of the review of each child's progress, and may be more useful than trying to decide whether the disability continues to be "permanent".

9. Confidentiality.

How will the authority ensure that the information on the register is protected? This may be necessary, not only with other professionals, but also with firms selling aids and adaptations.

Clearly, all departments involved will have to agree a policy of confidentiality about information exchange between them. They must then establish who is to be responsible for informing parents and children about the policy, about procedures and accountability if the policy is breached.

VIII. RACIAL ORIGIN OF CHILDREN IN NEED

"Every local authority shall, in making any arrangements -
(a)   for the provision of day care within their area; or
(b)   designed to encourage persons to act as local authority foster parents,
have regard to the different racial groups to which children within their area who are in need belong." sch 2(11)

This duty is linked to the provision of particular services, and without being explicit, gives support for the practice of same-race placements with foster carers and childminders, and of ethnic monitoring of nursery staff. It is unclear why a similar connection with the provision of residential services is not included; an authority wanting to implement the spirit of the legislation would want to extend the principle to all its establishments, and to any other agency with whom they have placed a child.

This duty is unequivocal - in other words, there are no "let out clauses" such as: "take reasonable steps to" or "as far as is practicable".

PERSONAL EXERCISE

*   Define for yourself your own ethnic origin, *(see glossary)* and that of a child in your family or who is close to you.

*   If you were applying for day care in your area, how would you know that the authority had had regard to that child's ethnic origin? In what practical ways would this be demonstrated to you, and to the child?

Some practical implications

1. Ethnic monitoring

The duty contained in sch.2(1) is to identify the extent of children in need in the area. In order to take this further and establish their racial origin, an authority must either:

1   introduce blanket policies of "in need" criteria based on ethnicity, or

2   be able to identify each individual child and her or his ethnic origin.

This duty cannot be carried out without the extensive application of ethnic monitoring of:

1   all children currently receiving services from the local authority,

2   all children in need in the area, and

3   by logical extension, all the foster carers, childminders, nursery staff and residential workers employed by and applying to the authority, in the context of:

4   accurate knowledge about the ethnic composition of the whole area.

An excellent short introduction to ethnic record keeping was written by Shama Ahmed in "Race and Social Work: a guide to training." (12) In answering some of the more common concerns and queries, she refutes both the possibility that identification could be used to disadvantage minority ethnic groups (it is already prevalent, she says) and the opposite fear that they might receive an unduly large amount of

resources. She points out, and we have seen from other research (13), that minority ethnic families are amongst those living in the most difficult conditions in the country and have least access to support services. At the same time they are likely to receive a disproportionate amount of attention in matters of social control, particularly in com-Ahmed offers some useful guidelines for the recording of information, which include:

*   **Don't** record nationality; not only is this fairly useless information for the purposes of a local authority, but it is also perceived as hostile and very threatening to families who may think that their immigration status is being questioned.

*   **Do** break down the word "Asian" ; also Latin American and others into more meaningful categories.

*   **Do** ask white clients too.

*   **Do** respect a client's origins as well as place of birth.

There are more suggestions in the book which could provide an interesting and useful exercise for your family centre, team or area team meeting to study and apply.

Simply recording information does not guarantee good or even improved practice regarding the provision of appropriate and high quality services for minority ethnic children. It needs to be supported by, amongst other factors:

*   a coherent statement of organisational values and objectives with an implementation strategy

*   an understanding about why the information is required so that it can be clearly explained to members of the public

*   monitoring of individual and general provision as part of the whole process

*   dissemination of the information to all staff

*   the expectation of changed aims, objectives, resource allocation and practice as a result

*   knowledge of how the Children Act further encourages anti-racist practice.

2. *Publicity re foster care and day care recruitment.*

As the duty states that this information gathering is in relation to making arrangements for the provision of day care and to encourage people to become foster carers, there are implications for the policy and practice of every homefinding/adoption and fostering/day care section. If they have not yet fully taken on the relevance and significance of ethnic monitoring and of recruitment which encourages appropriate carers, then this is a clear message that the planning for this must begin well in advance of the implementation date.

**TEAM EXERCISE
-
FOSTERING SECTIONS**

* What is your current policy and practice regarding the recruitment of black and minority ethnic carers?

* Is your policy written down, and does it have the approval and support of your senior management?

* How do you know whether you are recruiting carers of the same ethnic background as the children who need your service?

* Are you able to project future need as a result of demographic information of your area?

* If you need more information or advice, contact the National Foster Care Association or British Agencies for Adoption and Fostering.

(NB.- a note about the use of the words "foster parents/ carers". It is a pity that the Government failed to take up the National Foster Carers' Association's and others' proposals to use the word carer instead of parent. It would have signalled a conscious move away from the notion of substitute parenting, which would have been in keeping with the Act. Social work agencies may want to make this change themselves in their own child care policy documents and other material in order to clarify their changing philosophy.)

Chapter 2

*Social Work &
the Community*

1. **From paternalism to participation:** involving people in social services
S.Croft and P.Beresford, Open Services Project/Joseph Rowntree Foundation 1990

2. as above, no.1

3. **Key Facts**
National council for one-parent families

4. as above, chapter 1 no.11

5. as above, chapter 1 nos.16-37, and
Social services for black people: service or lip service?
A.Ahmad, Race Equality Unit, National Institute of Social Work 1988

6. Equality Now

7. as above, Chapter 1 no.19

8. **Open to complaints: guidelines for social services complaints procedures**
L.Berry and N.Doyle, NISW/ National Consumer Council 1988

9. **Consultation Paper no.17:**
Representations
D.o.H. 1990

10. **The Children Act 1989 Guidance and Regulations Volume 2:**
Family support, day care and educational provision for young children
D.o.H. 1991

11. **The Children Act 1989. Priorities for management information**
Social Information Systems 1990

12. as above, Chapter 1 no. 36

13. **Commission for Racial Equality publications: for details, see:**
Bibliography - social work, racism and black communities
ed. N.Ahmad, REU/NISW 1990

CHAPTER 3
SOCIAL WORK AGENCIES AND THE ACT

PRINCIPLES OF THE ACT

Children are generally best looked after within their families.	Parents and guardians retain parental responsibility and work in partnership with the LA.	No court order to be made unless better than making no order at all.	The child's welfare is the court's paramount consideration.	Orders available to protect children and avoid unwarranted intervention in family life.

DUTIES AND POWERS

Identify children in need, safeguard and promote their welfare .. within their families where consistent. s.17(1)	Provide a range and level of appropriate services. s.17(1)	Consult child, parent, those with parental responsibility and others whom the agency considers relevant when making decisions about child. s.22
Have regard to child's race, religion, culture and language when making decisions about children being looked after. s.22	Set up representations and complaints procedure and publicise its existence. s.26	Use orders under Parts IV and V if child suffering or likely to suffer significant harm. ss.31,43,44

PRINCIPLES AND PRACTICE GUIDE

No.1	No.4	No.5	No.7
Children and young people and their parents should all be considered as individuals with particular needs and potentialities.	A child's age, sex, health, personality, race, culture and life experiences are all relevant to any consideration of needs and vulnerability and have to be taken into account when planning or providing help.	There are unique advantages for children in experiencing normal family life in their own birth family and every effort should be made to preserve the child's home and family links.	The development of a working partnership with parents is usually the most effective route to providing supplementary or substitute care for their children.

EQUALITY ISSUES

Attitudes towards "the family" - the influence of institutional, societal, and personal belief and experience on assessment and planning.	Skills and knowledge available to accurately consult with child, relatives and others.	Ability to take into account the factors of race, culture, language and religion.	Ability to understand the effect of disability on the whole family.	Openness to working in partnership; developing a combination of anti-discriminatory policies; commitment to guaranteed resource provision; support to enable staff to work with confidence.

CHAPTER THREE
SOCIAL WORK AND FAMILIES

I. RESPECT FOR DIFFERENT FAMILY LIFESTYLES

1. *Family diversity and change*

In every area of the country, no matter how homogeneous its inhabitants may appear, there is a wealth of diversity in households and family lives. Some of that variety of experience may be easily visible, particularly in the inner cities, with their rapid population growth and mobility. In smaller towns and rural districts, where change comes more slowly, there may be an identifiable regional language or accent; they may share a common understanding or view about local traditions and values.

Family life, however, is changing everywhere. In the process, we are beginning to learn to challenge what we think an average family is all about:

FACT BITE (1):   1988 -   1/4 of all households were single person households

Marriage is no longer viewed in terms of long term security, and many parents choose not to marry:

FACT BITE (2):   1989 -   27% children born outside marriage
                      1989 -   37% all first marriages end in divorce

Black and minority ethnic families are in every region of the country, many having settled many generations ago:

FACT BITE (3):   1988 -   at least 9 out of every 10 minority ethnic children under 10 were born in the UK;
                      1988 -   black and minority ethnic citizens form 4.7% of the population.

Many women are raising their children alone, or are not living with the children's father:

FACT BITE (4):   1988 -   1 in every 7 families with dependent children is a single-parent family
                      1988 -   9 out of 10 lone parents are women

Roles defined by gender have changed:

FACT BITE (5):   1983 -   only 8% of the male workforce supported a non-earning wife and two children.

Many families are raising children who have a disability:

FACT BITE (6):   1989 -   there were 360,000 children with disabilities living in Britain.

(For all references, see end of chapter)

2. Social work assumptions about family life

Social workers, along with all others in the community, are subject to societal and media pressure to support the mythical notion of the existence of an average or normal family, along with its particular characteristics and lifestyle. This message is reinforced through much of their training and texts, and by powerful "workplace wisdom". In contrast, there is a growing body of feminist social work literature and work by black writers and others which is challenging these stereotypes. (see reading list for Chapter 1)

Why do these preoccupations matter, and what is their relevance to developing anti-discriminatory practice within the Children Act?

Social workers' assumptions, attitudes and beliefs about family life fundamentally affect the way in which we carry out our jobs, because the nature, purpose and viability of the families with whom we work is central to our task. This means that social work policy and practice must raise such attitudes and beliefs to a conscious level in order to make clear, both to workers and public, the basis on which the work is being carried out.

Policy documents, for example, may contain statements such as:

" *By family, we include a range of structures, not purely the two-parent, biological, nuclear family.*"

or:

"*To remember that there are many interpretations of 'normality' in family life..*"

or:

"*Recognising children's rights to a secure and permanent set of relationships should not be taken to mean that only the relatively closed nuclear family is an acceptable environment for children to grow up in.*" (7)

or, from the Principles and Practice Guide:

"*Although some basic needs are universal, there can be a variety of ways of meeting them. Patterns of family life differ according to culture, class and community and these differences should be respected and accepted. There is no one, perfect way to bring up children and care must be taken to avoid judgements and stereotyping*" (8)

CHECKPOINT:

Do you have such a statement in your agency's child care policy document? It may be argued that it is implicit. However, a clear, unequivocal statement recognising the value and strength of many different kinds of families will encourage and support positive practice.

On a practice level, social workers should be clear about their attitudes to the families living in our area, including their beliefs about the validity of those families' lifestyles. This agenda, which we all carry around with us, defines every piece of work undertaken with children. Nobody begins an assessment from a neutral starting point, and everyone needs to acknowledge how their agenda affects:

* the information asked / not asked for

* who is routinely included / excluded from assessments

* perceptions about family lifestyle

* judgements about good enough parenting

* what interventions/services are necessary.

3. Families and the Children Act

There are several ways in which the Children Act enables practitioners to think differently in relation to family structures and lifestyles. Here are four of them:

(a)   the concept of parental responsibility (sections 2-4);

(b)   the definition of family in Part III (s. 17(10));

(c)   the duty to consider racial origin, religious persuasion, cultural and linguistic backgrounds (s. 22(5) & sch. 2(11));

(d)   the duties and powers to promote the contact and involvement of relatives and other significant people, in addition to parents (sch.2(15)).

Additionally, the Act intends to support the autonomy and authority of family life by:

*   the principle of minimal court intervention (the presumption of no order, s.1(5);

*   the principle of supporting families to care for their children (the welfare duty s.17(1));

*   the principle of placing children with or near their relatives or friends and returning them to them as soon as possible (placement duties s.23(6)).

(a) Parental responsibility

This is an important new concept in child care legislation. It reflects a move away from the notion of a parent's rights over a child, or over a child's property, and towards an acceptance that modern parents have a collection of responsibilities towards youngsters which generally diminish as they grow older. Whereas previously only the biological or married parents could lay claim to rights over a child, and men were presumed to be the natural guardians of their legitimate children, the situation will now be that:

* all mothers and those fathers married before the birth automatically acquire parental responsibility;

* unmarried fathers may acquire it either by agreement with the mother or by court order;

* others may acquire it through a residence, care or emergency protection order, adoption or guardianship (limited powers). This would include co-habitees, grandparents, foster carers, the local authority and others.

The significance of the concept is two-fold:

i) parental responsibility can be shared by a number of people in respect of the same child at the same time, and

ii) it is retained after divorce and care orders are granted. Mothers and married fathers never lose their parental responsibility, except by adoption or death; others may lose it by application to the court for revocation or by discharging a court order.

Throughout the Act there are references to the ways in which parents and those with parental responsibility must be consulted, notified or otherwise involved in decision making by the local authority and the courts, and ways in which they may exert their authority. This means that all practitioners, including those caring for children on a daily basis must be fully informed about the legal status of different adults in respect of a particular child, and are clear about the significance of that status.

"Parental responsibility" can be welcomed in that it broadens the legal concept of parenting to reflect the reality in many families, which is that the tasks involved in raising children are shared by a number of people, not necessarily the most significant of whom are the biological parents. The concept does not, however, assist the recognition of non-biological lesbian and gay parents who may not apply for parental responsibility, as may unmarried fathers, but may only acquire it through a residence order application. Given the prejudice shown towards biological lesbian and gay parents (9) it is unlikely that any will voluntarily bring themselves before the courts. At this stage, the status of sperm and egg donors, and those to whom they have donated, remains unclear.

Additional concerns can be noted regarding the position of some women, particularly young women, who may be vulnerable to unwanted, continuing involvement with the fathers of their children. These are women who may not want to pursue maintenance applications for a variety of reasons, and some may have their benefits reduced as a result. Financial pressure may force them into agreeing to disclose the names of men who may, in turn, decide to apply to court for parental responsibility or contact. Once granted, the fathers will be able to act independently of the mothers (s. 2(7)), and are entitled to be consulted, for example about the provision of accommodation by a local authority. Given the power imbalance between women and men, this may act against the interests of women who wish to remain single parents.

Practitioners will need to be wary of any attempts to view the exercise of parental responsibility as either financial maintenance or accountability for children's criminal acts. Although both of these issues are highly important to all parents, the Children Act does not cover them, and there is

no direct legal connection between them and the granting or refusal of parental responsibility. The court will, of course, have to remember to make the child's welfare its paramount consideration when deciding any contested case.

TEAM EXERCISE

* In your team's current caseload, who has parental rights over the children? Are there any cases in which you are unsure of someone's status? Do you feel that this legal status is a fair reflection of the relationship between the children and the adults who are most important to them?

* What could happen to the status of all those people under the Children Act? Are there people whom you would advise to apply for parental responsibility, perhaps through an application for a residence order?

* What do you think are the pros and cons of these changes?

(b) Definition of family

There is only one description of family in the Act, and that comes in Part III, s.17(10). It is in relation to the people to whom a local authority (or other agency or individual carrying out its functions under Part III) may provide a service. It states:

"Any service... may be provided for the family of a particular child in need or for any member of his family, if it is provided with a view to safeguarding or promoting the child's welfare." s.17, 3.

"...'family', in relation to such a child, includes any person who has parental responsibility for the child and any other person with whom he has been living." s.17,10.

This definition therefore includes non-rela-

tives who are living with a child, but excludes others who may be very significant. For example, the sibling of a child in need may not be living in the same household, but nearby with an aunt. Unless the sibling meets the criteria of a child in need, she or he and the aunt are not entitled as of right to the provision of a service under Part III. It will be up to local authorities to ensure that unduly narrow definitions of "in need" do not limit them to inappropriately restrictive services.

(c) The racial origin of children in need.

You will risk acting illegally if you work on an unchecked assumption about children's racial origin. In two main areas - that is day care and the provision of accommodation - the racial origin of children in need must be given due consideration: sch.2(11) and s.22(5). As this cannot be done without knowledge of that racial origin, this information must be clearly established at the outset. The potential for making this the starting point for much more appropriate and sensitive service provision is there.

(See Chapter 3 p72 for further discussion of this point)

CHECKPOINT:

* What kind of ethnic monitoring is currently underway or planned in your agency? How can you get this information?

* What do you and your colleagues do now to get this information when you are meeting new clients?

* How is the family involved in this, and are they told how, why and where the information is kept?

(d) Other relatives and significant adults.

"Wider families matter as well as parents - especially siblings and grandparents. Family friends may play an important part. Black families in particular may have 'aunties' and 'uncles' who have a close relationship with a child without being blood relatives. Links with individuals and the wider community can and should be maintained."

"Continuity of relationships is important, and attachments should be respected, sustained and developed." (10)

Various duties and powers within the Act recognise the significance and value of people who form part of children's wider networks; not all of these are relatives. Examples are :

-"Before making any decision with respect to a child whom they are looking after, or proposing to look after, a local authority shall, so far as is reasonably practicable, ascertain the wishes and feelings of -
.. any other person whose wishes and feelings the authority consider to be relevant."
s. 22 (4)

- "Where a child is being looked after by a local authority, the authority shall, unless it is not reasonably practicable or consistent with his .welfare, endeavour to promote contact between the child and -
... any relative, friend or other person connected with him" sch.2(15)(c).

- "..where -
(a)   a child is being looked after by a local authority...
The authority may - make payments to -
... any relative, friend or other person connected with him,.." sch.2(16).

Whilst powers do not carry the same weight in law as duties (i.e. things you **may**, but do not **have** to do) at the same time an agency is expected to have regard to its powers to ensure the duty (for example, promoting contact) is met. This gives practitioners who

want to initiate and develop good practice with family and other networks, some practical supports for doing so.

PERSONAL EXERCISE

*   Think about a child or children with whom you are working at the moment. Do you know who their relatives, friends and any "person connected" are? How do you go about getting this information? Is there someone else who may be in a better position to ask about it?

*   How do you go about consulting with this group of people at the moment? Do you think that you will need to make any changes in your practice to satisfy the new duty?

*   If you have children in your care, list ways in which you could promote contact between them and the people you have identified. What are the obstacles which stop you doing this now? (This might include your beliefs about contact being harmful; no money in the budget to facilitate visits; thinking that there are more urgent things to do)

*   Discuss with your supervisor, or in your team, how you can get support to overcome those obstacles

---

Chapter 3

Social Work Agencies & Families

II. THE ASSESSMENT PROCESS

Whatever the overall relationship between a social work agency and the community it serves, the quality of the service is usually measured by individuals in terms of the personal contact with representatives of that agency and the work undertaken by them.

This section focuses on the earliest stages of that work: the assessment process. For reasons of space, it isn't possible to go into detail about the other essential stages of the work, including the planning, reviewing and ending. Assessments are perhaps particularly worthy of attention because they are so powerful: the purpose, the analysis, the process, the recommendations which result are the foundation on which subsequent work is carried out. For children and their families, access to or denial of services will depend on assessment, as will significant decisions about intervention, which may be unsought and unwelcome, in their lives.

Before looking at assessment duties and powers contained in the Children Act, and the ways in which they can support and require anti-discriminatory practice, it is important to think about the principles, experience and authority which practitioners bring to this work.

1. Why do assessments?

Each worker who carries out an assessment has in common the need to:

- find out information
- analyse situations
- make judgements
- define problems
- weigh up advantages and disadvantages
- find resources and abilities available to resolve problems
- suggest and carry out solutions.

2. When will you do them?

Under the Children Act, when are they to take place?

There are a number of legal requirements to make assessments. These are some examples:

Part I   preparing court reports using the s.1 checklist

Part II   preparing welfare reports for a s.8 order

Part III   deciding whether a child is a child in need, and meets the criteria for service provision

Part IV   deciding the extent and nature of harm with a view to instigating care proceedings

Part V   deciding whether an application is necessary to safeguard a child from immediate harm

Part VI   deciding whether a community home is suitable for different children

Parts VII, VIII and IX   deciding whether children accommodated elsewhere or being privately fostered are receiving adequate care to safeguard and promote their welfare

Part X   deciding whether a childminder is providing adequate day care.

3. On what basis are assessments carried out?

i)   the authority vested in the worker by virtue of the job and the responsibilities and powers it brings

ii)   the professional principles by which the worker is guided and which are informed by training and knowledge

iii) the worker's **personal identity** and **experience**, beliefs and attitudes which define much of what is brought to the assessment.

(i) Authority

The authority of the job can be equated with the power of the organisation, with the status of the job title and profession, the rank held and the legal powers conferred on the job holder. These benefits are very specific to different professionals; families have clear views about the relative roles and responsibilities of social workers, health visitors, the police and doctors, and the kind of assessment that such positions entitle each person to make. (This does not mean that it is always made clear in individual cases, and research has highlighted, for example, the problem of a failure to clarify the differing perspectives and aims held by worker and family.) (11)

Practitioners are the representatives of their organisations and this underlies the relationship made and sustained with families; the power implicit in this should not be underestimated or ignored - however friendly the worker, however well everyone gets on, the family will not forget that this helpful person also has the power to act, to withhold or provide services, to deregister them as carers of children, to remove children from them, to take them to court, to influence other professionals and perhaps even remove their liberty.

The power differential already referred to in the section on access to services operates here too. As we saw, some children and adults, particularly black and minority ethnic people, are unduly and negatively affected by the social control powers of social work organisations. On an individual basis, any such discriminatory use of authority cannot be separated from the discriminatory use of any additional power workers derive from other aspects of their identity .

(ii) Principles

The principles by which practitioners are expected to abide throughout the country are also partly defined by differences in professional aims and training. Doctors may put priority on being prepared to care for all sick people, regardless of their circumstances; police on upholding the law no matter who the law breaker; teachers on realizing the full potential of all children in their care. Social workers are likely to emphasise respect for each individual, the importance of providing security and self-esteem for children and helping families in trouble to overcome their difficulties and become self-sufficient.

Within these broad themes and aims of the profession there are enormous variations and interpretations of good practice. BASW has issued Codes of Practice, the Department of Health likewise (for example the Code of Practice on Access 1984) and most recently publishing Jane Rowe's Principles and Practice Guide on the Children Act. Rowe suggests that:

"It may be helpful to think of principles as the colours on a social work painter's palette to be used in the combinations and patterns required for each picture painted/child care case handled. Social workers need to be as familiar with the principles of good child care as painters are with the colours in their paint box."

She continues:

"Principles must never be applied blindly but used intelligently with common sense and sensitivity because it can be dangerous to overemphasise any one principle to the extent that others are ignored or flouted" (12)

Find nice principle to peut in front o there !

Chapter 3

Social Work Agencies & Families

(iii) Personal identity and experience

No social worker, doctor, teacher, solicitor or other person in a position of authority in our society arrives at their desk without bringing with them a whole collection of personal business which critically and directly affects their work. Our individual " baggage " goes with us all the time, on every visit, to every case conference and to every assessment. Our assessment work is as much a product of our own views and experience as it is of the information we gather. Part of the skill we need to employ is to recognise this and understand its influence on perceptions and decision making. In addition, our identity and behaviour affects the way in which clients and other workers perceive us; this will define some of the information they give us or ways in which they behave with us.

For example, a woman social worker recently highlighted (13) her difficulties in working with Bangladeshi boys who had been sexually abused; although she was herself Asian and spoke Bengali, she brought to work her female identity and western values and ideas which she said, made it very hard for boys and men to talk to her.

Many social workers are not as aware of their effect as she was, although there are men who are discussing with female colleagues how they can play an appropriate, supportive role in cases of sexual abuse or domestic violence to enable the women to do the direct work.

More subtle than gender, age or racial identities are the influences of personal experiences and beliefs. Social work students are taught during practice placement to learn how to put aside their own feelings of, for example, grief and anger about divorce in order to assist a client to deal with their own. What receives less attention are students' views and values about, for example, divorce in general: does the student believe that marriages should stay intact no matter what the circumstances; that divorce is not part of her or his cultural experience; that marriage is not a good thing; that there are societal influences which are responsible for causing marriage breakdown; that divorce makes a family dysfunctional; that men must support women financially after divorcing them?

Any of these beliefs - and we all hold some view about divorce - will crucially affect the way in which a practitioner assesses a family where divorce has happened, but this is rarely accounted for in recording assessment work, even though that record may be used in court proceedings to determine a child's or family's future. The s.1 checklist in the Act determines that such information be brought before the court to help them to determine what is best for the child, but there are no provisions for taking into account the beliefs and prejudices of the worker.

Looking at how practitioners may carry out assessment work with children and families under the Children Act forms the remainder of this chapter. Piecing together information about children's lives is rather like putting together a jigsaw; even though you may never find all the pieces, at some point you learn enough to see enough of the picture. Anti-discriminatory practice means asking for information in a way which makes real connections between those different pieces rather than try to force together bits that cannot fit, according to a pre-conceived notion of how the picture should turn out. The result can be very rewarding. This whole picture approach recognises the importance of viewing children in the context of their whole environment including the personal, psychological and familial, within their network of friends and community; as well as within their racial, cultural, gender, sexual, religious and class identity and as a person with or without disabilities. It also takes into account their experience in society as a whole and as individuals and members of different groups within that society.

3

Chapter

**Social Work
Agencies
& Families**

III. THE IDENTIFICATION OF CHILDREN IN NEED

- some practice issues

In Chapter 2 we saw that each local authority is to identify the extent of children in need within their area and to prioritise those needs and provide services accordingly. (Schedule 2(1)) No authority is expected to meet all the needs of all the children in its area. Each one will be devising its own criteria to form the basis of policy and procedures for the guidance of staff who will have the task of locating such children and applying the criteria.

In assisting policy makers to prepare an "audit" of need based on a profile of the area and communities within it, an opportunity exists to highlight at local council and national level the true needs of all children, before targeting those for whom that authority intends to provide a service. This is an essential task in developing anti-discriminatory policies, before tackling the inevitable and painful job of priority-setting.

Social workers experience different pressures to their managers in making assessments about which children are in need.

In addition to:

* the legal framework;

* agency policy and interpretation of "in need";

* budgetary constraints;

they will experience:

* the stress of carrying out a policy which excludes considerable numbers of children;

* understanding the legal definitions and limits of their actions;

* dealing with the anger and distress of families who are excluded from the criteria for service provision;

* explaining the effects of departmental policies to colleagues from other departments.

Within the context of these difficult circumstances, workers who are looking to continue or develop their anti-discriminatory practice may consider these issues:

1. Is your starting point for identifying a child in need that of the child and family, or of your agency?

In other words, in beginning the assessment process outlined in the introduction, is your purpose simply to assess whether the child meets the criteria in s.17(10) or (11)? If so, this will clarify but also limit the information you seek, the problem or need you define and the solutions and resources available to meet it. In all families, there are likely to be a complex group of factors which interlink and don't fit into pre-defined criteria. If your assessment is family-led rather than agency-led, what differences are likely to result in your definition of the problem and the subsequent service delivery?

2. A consequence of undertaking assessments in a way which uses the family's definition of their difficulties (including any differences they have between them) is that their views and concerns are respected and legitimised.

Making this a conscious part of the work is an important way of valuing and working positively with people, and beginning your relationship with the assumption that you both have something to offer in terms of working out the problem and its solution.

Unfortunately, this is not the experience of many families who are assessed by social work agencies; many are pre-judged because of their skin colour, their poverty or some other aspect of their identity or lifestyle. Misunderstandings which subsequently occur can have severely damaging effects.

3. Maintaining a clear distinction between whether the assessment is about:

(a) deciding if the child is in need of services under Part III of the Act, or
(b) deciding if the child is in need of protection under Part IV or Part V.

It is well known that in many hard-pressed areas, the only work being undertaken is that of child protection, and much of that is only with the most extreme and serious of cases. It is vitally important, however, that the criteria for services under Part III are not simply that a child may be at risk of significant harm or neglect without such provision. (Such a restriction may also lead to an authority acting illegally with reference to the definition of children in need.) If this were to be the case, then everyone who approached the department for anything from help with transport costs to visit a child in accommodation, to a part-time childminder, would undergo an assessment to decide whether their child is at risk. If this is a necessary intervention, then the child protection procedures should be invoked and the reasons, process and possible outcome explained to the family. Additionally, because all children with disabilities are included in the definition of children in need, it would imply that all those children would also be considered in need of protection unless, as a category, they were exempted.

4. Maintaining a further distinction between your agency's definition of the extent of children "in need" and the criteria you are to apply for access to services.

Practitioners must remember that their authorities will not be expected to meet all the needs of all the children in their area, and will have set priorities within their definitions of the extent of need. This means that there will be situations where a child fits the definition but is still not to be supplied with a service. Workers may want to check whether their authority's priorities properly reflect the real needs of the community, including those who traditionally have least access and least power.

Managers and practitioners have, understandably, different viewpoints and responsibilities around this issue. A difficult situation arises where agency policy appears to discriminate against some people and agency employees must decide what action to take.

ORGANISATION EXERCISE

* Examine your local authority's new child care policy statement together with their criteria for service provision. If you believe that this is in any way discriminatory, what do you think

* you

* your manager

* a member of the public

* an elected member

} could do

IV. SERVICES TO THE FAMILY

"Any service provided by a local authority in the exercise of its functions conferred on them by this section may be provided for the family of a particular child in need or for any member of his family if it is provided with a view to safeguarding or promoting his welfare." s. 17(3)

The implications of this power are positive, in that the principle is established that a separate service can be provided for the adults or siblings in the family of a child in need. This could be wide ranging, for example, drug abuse counselling, literacy class, a holiday. The disadvantage lies in the description of "family" which, for the purposes of Part III, is:" any person who has parental responsibility for the child and any other person with whom he has been living." s. 17(10)

This means that there is no power or duty to provide services to, for example, siblings living with grandparents elsewhere, although it does mean that non-related members of the household, such as a parent's partner, would be included.

V. STANDARDS OF HEALTH AND DEVELOPMENT

According to s.17(10), services should be provided for children who cannot achieve or maintain a reasonable standard of physical, intellectual, social and behavioural development and physical and mental health, without the provision of those services. Failure to achieve such a standard in any of these areas may be a way of recognising a child in need and serious failure may be grounds for considering care proceedings.

Social workers are unlikely to be sufficiently knowledgeable in all these areas to be able alone, or in their teams, to fully assess any child's health and development . Under the Children Act, as previously, they will consult a broad range of co-professionals to gather the necessary information. Relevant colleagues will be found, for example, in the child health services. There may be link workers with families whose use of English is limited. If a child suffers from a specific illness or has a particular medical condition, such as asthma or sickle cell anaemia, every effort should be made to get appropriate advice from those used to working with these conditions and able to fully explain the implications.

Social workers are likely to be skilled in using some kind of standard assessment format, such as the "orange book" i.e. "Protecting children", issued by the D.o.H.(14). This includes much detailed guidance such as the development progress chart by Mary Sheridan (p.88) and the needs of children outlined by Christine Cooper (p.33). The book makes it clear that assessments must include gathering information from the child her/himself, the parent(s) and other important relatives or members of the household.

Issues for social workers in undertaking this process are common to all assessment processes, and some of these are looked at in more detail at the beginning of this chapter. Placing the assessment in a broad context, which routinely includes socio-economic, ethnic, cultural and disability cross-references, is essential.

Example no.1:

a family may live in chronic poverty, not as a result of "a generally chaotic lifestyle" (orange book, p.61), but as a result of having been in receipt of state benefits for an extended period. Poverty substantially reduces a parent's ability to provide adequately for children's physical and mental health. In addition, the effects of a detrimental diet, poor housing, inadequate heating and constant lack of cash on an adult's abilities to deal with further pressures must be carefully included. In any assessment, the family may be spending money on items, such as cigarettes, alcohol or pets, that you may consider to be unacceptable and "proof" that it is the behaviour of the family that is the cause of the poverty rather than employment prospects or benefit levels. However, what you are seeing may be one expression of how this family copes with an unacceptable situation.

Example no.2:

a family should usually be asked about their ethnic and cultural backgrounds and religious affiliation. Whatever information emerges is not then a problematical area to be dealt with, but is relevant information which will be taken into account in your assessment. What may arise, however, is a problem which the family have experienced as a result of societal ignorance or racism or specifically the prejudice of an individual worker. This external pressure may have produced a reaction in one or more of the family members which an unwary worker may record inaccurately. For example, an Asian woman with small children who appears withdrawn and isolated and whose children rarely go out may not be a stereotypically submissive wife, but rather someone who has racist neighbours and cannot leave home without experiencing hostility and rejection.

In recording their own perceptions and observations, social workers need also to record the standards against which they are measuring, show the family this measure-

ment and check whether:

a)   they are in agreement about what is a reasonable standard in the first place, and

b)   whether their perceptions differ, and if so, how. For example, a lively, chatty three year old who constantly interrupts visitors with a stream of questions may be seen as rude and disobedient by some people and delightfully assertive by others.

The information a worker gains will not only depend on their own experience, ethnic and cultural backgrounds and political views, but also on how they are viewed by the child and family, both personally and as a representative of the agency. A poor white working class family, for example, may instinctively distrust the ability of a young, white, middle class worker to fully appreciate the nature of their problems; a Caribbean family allocated a Caribbean worker may have precisely the same problem which may be exacerbated by the necessity of placing the black worker in a position of power in relation to them and as identified with a white organisation.

If both workers ask these families questions which are based on an agency assumption that "normal" family life is to be modelled on white, middle class, nuclear families, then both will find the questions inappropriate, the answers unhelpful and their own observations distorted.

Chapter 3

**Social Work
Agencies
& Families**

VI. ASSESSMENT WORK WITH CHILDREN WITH DISABILITIES AND THEIR FAMILIES

In some circumstances, social workers will need to extend their assessment skills in order to work with children with special needs. Children with disabilities will be amongst them. They form a group about whom many social workers have little direct knowledge, as in most social service departments there are specialists who liaise closely with their colleagues in health and education departments. Under the Children Act, particular references are made to children with disabilities; there are definitions, duties and services which are applicable to them over and above those which apply to all children.

In this section, we are going to highlight these duties and services, in order to explore how social workers might positively use their new powers and carry out their new tasks.

The definition

In the Act, children with disabilities are referred to as "disabled". It says:

"For the purposes of this Part (i.e. Part III), a child is disabled if he is blind, deaf or dumb or suffers from mental disorder of any kind or is substantially or permanently handicapped by illness, injury or congenital deformity or such other disability as may be prescribed;" s. 17(11)

All children who meet this criteria are automatically considered to be "children in need". This means that they will receive services which are part of mainstream child care provisions, duties and powers. However, local authorities are still not obliged to meet all the needs of all these children. There will be priority setting and access to services will be conditional.

The definition has the same meaning as in the National Assistance Act 1948 which still applies to adults. This is intended to facilitate the identification of future adults who may require services from the local authority, and improve long term planning. It is also compatible with the working definition used in the Chronically Sick and Disabled Persons Act and with various benefit entitlement criteria. However, the definition has been criticised as old fashioned and limited, in continuing to define children by their disease or handicap, rather than seeing them firstly, as children and

secondly, as people with special needs, with strengths they have developed and limitations placed on them by their disability. As people are affected so variably within each area of disability, an assessment of the extent to which functioning is affected may have been more appropriate.

In the U.S.A., the term "developmental disorder" is widely used, with the emphasis on needs rather than deficits:

" A developmental disability is a severe, chronic disability which:

* is attributed to a mental or physical impairment or a combination of mental and physical impairments;

* is manifested before the person attains the age twenty-two;

* is likely to continue indefinitely;

* results in substantial functional limitations in three or more of the following areas of major life activity: self-care, receptive and expressive language, learning, mobility, self-direction, capacity for independent living and economic self-sufficiency; and

* reflects the person's need for a combination and sequence of special inter-disciplinary or generic care, treatment or other services which are of lifelong or extended duration and are individually planned and co-ordinated."

(The Development Disabilities Act (1984) s. 102)

In Britain, the concept of "special needs" has been accepted in education assessment and provision, again emphasising the importance of looking at children's strengths as well as weaknesses. Social workers and others interested in this would find Circular 22/89 on this subject from the Department of Education and Science both easy to read and very helpful.

In addition to these problems of definition, the language used in the Children Act is regarded as archaic and offensive.

" The language of disability has been created by a largely able-bodied society. Words used in the context of disability tend to be negative. ...We talk about people as being 'weak-hearted', 'short-sighted', 'deaf to reason'.. Through words like these, people build up a picture of disability as a negative thing, a problem."

" People with disabilities are campaigning to be accorded the same respect and rights as able-bodied people. To this end they are devising new terms which stress their many strengths rather than focus on their weaknesses. 'Differently-abled' is one such term". (15)

CHECKPOINT

What language is used in your office to describe people with disabilities?

What is your own definition of the words "handicap" and "disability"?

Can you replace the words used in the Act's definition with positive ones?

The purpose

The local authority's duty behind any service provision to children with disabilities will be the same as for all children "in need", which is:

"(a) to safeguard and promote the welfare of children within their area who are in need; and

(b) so far as is consistent with that duty, to promote the upbringing of such children by their families," s. 17,1 (1)

As with all children in need, there is an underlying assumption that they are generally best cared for within their own families. Assessment and services should, therefore, both be geared to to this end, and neither should overlook the significance of factors other than disability within the family. A full assessment which includes all the information necessary to establish the extent of need and related factors in the child, family, significant others and the community should be undertaken. There is provision in sch.2,3 to undertake assessments of children with disabilities at the same time as those being arranged under different legislation, such as the Education Act 1981. Whilst it is sensible to reduce for both children and their carers the number of professionals pursuing separate procedures and possibly duplicating questions and tests, social workers must guard against assuming that all relevant information has been gathered. Specialist health and education workers, for example, may not normally enquire about links with other important people such as relatives not living in the household, supportive friends, religious or spiritual advisers. They may have given advice about which benefits to claim, but be unaware of a large debt problem, redundancy or the effect of high interest rates on the family's ability to cope financially. These professionals will also need to ask specifically about ethnicity, culture and religion, in addition to language.

That said, however, there is no doubt that the stressful effects on a family of caring for a child with a severe, long term disability are often better understood by health and education staff than by most social workers. This stress manifests itself in a number of ways as already outlined and can include material, physical and emotional worries. Practitioners need to develop expertise in recognising these effects, the strengths and problems which arise and be able to distinguish what is related to the disability and what is not.

Chapter 3

Social Work Agencies & Families

How to carry out the welfare duty

Local authorities are required to achieve their aims by:
"providing a range of services appropriate to those children's needs" s. 17(1)

The range and level of services appropriate to these children must take account of them in the context of:

(a)   themselves as individuals, with an ethnic and cultural identity, character, personality, range of experience, and a level of developmental abilities and needs;

(b)   their families, with their identity, networks, place in the community, strengths and weaknesses, and in relation to caring for a child with a disability; and

(c)   their local and wider community, including their supports and social life, their peer group and school and also how they identify themselves and are identified by others; the effects of prejudice about their disability, the added possibility of other prejudices such as sexism or racism; how they see their future and how others see it.

In order to meet the additional duties, and use the extra powers that they have in relation to children with disabilities:

"Every local authority shall open and maintain a register of disabled children within their area" (sch.2(2))

"Every local authority shall provide services designed -

(a)   to minimise the effect on disabled children within their area of disabilities; and

(b)   to give such children the opportunity to lead lives which are as normal as possible." (sch.2(6))

"Where a local authority provide accommodation for a child whom they are looking after and who is disabled, they shall, so far as is reasonably practicable, secure that the accomodation is not unsuitable to his particular needs." (s.23(8))

Leading a normal life

Some of the issues involved in setting up the register in a sensitive and open way were discussed in Chapter 2 (p40), and we shall look at the question of suitable accommodation in Chapter 4 (p.118).

The remaining, clumsily-worded duties unfortunately give the impression that children with disabilities cannot lead normal lives without the provision of services, and seem to imply that they should be striving to achieve some quality of life which children without disabilities already enjoy. When making assessments of need, of possible harm or neglect, and of services required, workers will need to challenge their assumptions about what they think children feel is appropriate for them "to minimise the effect of their disabilities". Attempts should be made to avoid simply minimising the effect of that disability on their lives, without checking this with them first. Many children will learn as they grow, what they are enabled to do, can do better, or can even only do, as a result of their particular disability. This positive and essential belief in their different abilities can be ignored, misunderstood or undermined by careless assessment work.

TEAM EXERCISE

*   List all the children you know, including family and friends, who have a disability of some kind ; include those with behavioural or learning difficulties.

*   How would you assess whether they were leading normal lives? Would you assess black children and white children, and girls and boys differently, and if so why and how? Does your team have a common view of what is normal for these children?

*   Think up another list of children you know, who do not have a disability. Do they lead normal lives? What different assessment criteria have you used for the two groups?

*   Discuss the implications of trying to carry out an assessment and decide on appropriate services, based on the criteria you have used.

At the beginning of the chapter, we listed some of the different kinds of assessments which practitioners will be undertaking, using the duties and powers in the Children Act. There are several issues of particular importance to children with disabilities which arise from this work. Here are some of them:

1.   Consulting with children who have hearing and speech difficulties.

2.   Giving due consideration to their wishes and feelings.

3.   Children of "sufficient understanding".

4.   Independent representation for children with disabilities.

1. Consultation

There is a wide variety of children who find it difficult to hear what is said to them, or to respond verbally. This is not always due to a physical handicap, but may have arisen through, for example, an emotional or mental disorder. There are few workers within area teams, day care or family centres, juvenile justice or home-finding teams, who are able to use sign language or other means of communication. Apart from specialist establishments or projects, these children can be cut off from having any confidential discussions with a worker of their choice, and may resist talking to the one or two people who can sign, for reasons such as gender or ethnic incompatibility. They are also unable to use the increasingly popular telephone advice lines; although the recent addition of a new line for children in boarding schools was seen to be of great benefit for a group of isolated and vulnerable children, it is of no use to the especially vulnerable, who cannot communicate by telephone.

CHECKPOINT

*   How many workers in your team/office can sign?

*   Is there any training for those who want to learn?

*   How else can you learn to communicate with children who cannot talk to you?

There is growing concern about children with a speech or hearing impediment and who have been physically or sexually abused.

2. Due consideration to wishes and feelings

There are clear duties throughout the Act to not only listen to childrens' views, but also to pay attention to them. It is the first factor in a court's "welfare checklist" s.1,(3). Whose

Chapter 3

Social Work Agencies & Families

job is it likely to be to find out these wishes and feelings and decide how to incorporate them into the work? How has this previously happened? Again, this was probably the task of specialist carers and workers, as well as family members. However, when local authorities begin their new inspection duties of residential establishments, and when they are obliged to hold statutory reviews on children in accommodation, non-specialist workers will have to develop new skills in working with these family members and carers, in order to form their own judgements. Specialists, for their part, will be required to show how they have reached their view of what the child wants. Multi-disciplinary assessments are already common practice in all areas where health, education and social work laws and provisions overlap. What is new here is the role that the local authorities will have to develop in order to meet their welfare duties towards children with disabilities.

TEAM EXERCISE

*   Find an example of a multi-disciplinary assessment of a child with a disability. What was the main purpose and focus of the assessment and how was it carried out? What part did the family play?

*   If this child was your responsibility, how would you ensure that her or his wishes and feelings had been a) ascertained, and b) given due consideration?

*   If you decide that you would have needed someone from outside your team to help you with this, arrange a meeting with her or him to discuss how you might go about it, and what are the likely implications for your future practice and procedures.

---

3. Children of "sufficient understanding"

Under the Children Act, children who are judged to be of sufficient understanding are able to:

(a)   refuse to be medically or psychiatrically examined or otherwise assessed
(s.43(8) s.44(7) s.38(6))

(b)   apply for leave to make an application for a section 8 order
(s.10(8))

(c)   apply for leave to make an application to end a parental responsibility order
(s. 4(4))

These are new and significant powers but the extent to which children and young people are able to exercise them will depend on the extent to which they are given the support and information to do so by adults close to them - the family members, social workers, guardians *ad litem*, solicitors and health and education workers, such as educational psychologists and paediatricians. Children with disabilities are open to a certain level of discrimination in this respect which goes beyond that experienced by all children who are in contact with large welfare organisations.

This includes:

(a)   ignorance of their level of understanding , which may be attributable to the worker's inability to communicate satisfactorily;

(b)   ignorance of the effect of their disability, which may be especially hard to judge with those with emotional and behavioural disorders;

(c)   failure to advise a child or young person fully of the implications of their decisions;

(d)   failure to give a clear commitment to

support the child in whatever decision is made, so that the child can follow it through with confidence; and

(e)   failure to take seriously the rights of these children to have access to the necessary information in a form they can understand.

Some organisations which represent the interests of children and young people being looked after will be preparing guides for them about these and other rights. Local authorities are themselves charged with this duty (s. 26(2)).

CHECKPOINT

*   How did your agency previously inform children of their rights?

*   Was this information made available to children with disabilities in writing, in their own first language and in any other form they can understand?

*   How did your policies and practice have to change in order for this to happen?

---

4. Independent representation

There are a number of circumstances in which children will require independent representation or advice, including in some assessment situations. It will be part of a social worker's list of resources to have the contact organisations which may act as a supporter or advocate. These may include: Voice for the Child in Care; Black and In Care: Independent Representation for Children in Need; National Association for Young People in Care; Albert Kennedy Trust.

How far do children with disabilities have access to these organisations? What happens if they want to contact them but cannot without assistance?

WORKING WITH THE FAMILIES OF CHILDREN WITH DISABILITIES

The principles of good practice which apply to all families are of course equally applicable to families who are caring for a child with a disability. There are other ways, however, in which these children and their families currently face discrimination from social work and other agencies, and which require particular attention:

*   failure to see the child as a whole person, by focusing on the disability and neglecting other important aspects of their identity, circumstances and life experience;

*   seeing the whole family as disabled ;

*   failure to recruit suitable foster carers;

*   lack of information given to children, young people and their families about services available within the organisation, in other agencies and from national or local self help groups;

*   allocation of the most inexperienced social workers;

*   failure to consult properly with the person with the disability;

*   poor communication and mistrust between professionals, resulting in unpredictable and unhelpful service

*   sending children a long distance from home because of lack of suitable provision locally;

*   failure to assess needs accurately so that inappropriate services are offered;

*   poor understanding of the amount of money needed to care for some children with disabilities;

*   grossly inadequate level of funding

Chapter 3

Social Work Agencies & Families

Chapter 3

Social Work Agencies & Families

available to support children within their own communities;

*   particularly poor level of service offered to black and minority ethnic children, who experience racism in addition to the difficulties outlined above; and

-    long delays and lack of support to families involved in legal proceedings, where a child was disabled in a medical or other accident.

One organisation has produced a leaflet and video which informs Asian families with children with learning difficulties how to seek help (16). They drew up a list of principles which should underpin service provision to them and other parents. This is what they said:

General principles for the development and guidance of services for families of children with special needs.

Published by the Early Support Action Group.

1. The overall concern of all services should be to meet the needs of both the child and his/her family as a whole, and not just the health and educational needs of the child.

2. All family members should be given the utmost respect as befits those who play the most important part in helping the child with special needs. They should always be treated with courtesy, dignity, honesty and understanding.

3. All professionals should work with parents in partnership and not take over from them.

4. The families' own resources and skills should be supported, facilitated and encouraged at all times and not inhibited in any way. Every effort should be made to foster their self-confidence and competence.

5. All professionals should listen carefully to each family and arrive at decisions made on the basis of explicit negotiation, therefore allowing for the individuality of families in terms of their needs, values, strengths, experience and beliefs.

6. Parents should have full access to information at all times, to use it if they choose.

7. Working with parents like this requires that explicit training on general psychological and interpersonal skills be provided for all professionals working in this area.

8. Full concern should be given to the interface between the organisation of services and the family, with the designation of one person from any of the voluntary and statutory services to work closely with the family on a regular basis to provide psychological, social and other support as necessary.

9. Support and help should begin as soon as a child is suspected of or diagnosed as having special needs, and should be continuous thereafter, if acceptable to the family.

10. This should be backed by a broad range of voluntary and statutory service options available to the family to help them meet their psychological, educational, medical, practical and financial needs. All options should be adequately publicised, resourced, organised and co-ordinated.

11. Services should be organised on an active multi-disciplinary basis, not dominated by the perceptions of one or two professionals, and should include parent representation at all levels of planning, organisation and decision-making. There should be full co-operation between the voluntary and statutory services, whose role should be complementary and clear.

12. There should be an explicit policy statement produced by each district describing the aims of services, their provision and organisation, with regular attempts to monitor and evaluate the extent to which their aims are achieved. Such information should be up-dated regularly.

The Action Group on Early Support consulted with a wide range of consumers and services. These principles of early support remind us of the importance of working sensitively and effectively with all families and the need to ensure that Asian families have full access to all local and statutory services. Further information is available from the Voluntary Council for Handicapped Children (address on page 17).

-reproduced with the kind permission of Phillipa Russell at the National Childrens' Bureau

There is one issue which we would like to look at in a bit more detail: the situation of black children with disabilities, including those for whom English is not their first language.

Black children and their families

In this section, we discuss in more detail some of the problems experienced by black children and their families who are subjected to assessments which are often racist, even though this may be unintentional. We will look at how workers can try to make use of the new legislation to undermine, confront and make unacceptable this behaviour. It could be argued that of all the black children whose racial identity, needs and development are ignored or dismissed by professionals, those with disabilites have the worst experience. Children and their families are in this position for a number of reasons, in which the disability and their ethnicity are closely interconnected.

These are some of the reasons:

1.   colour blindness
2.   integration and normalisation
3.   racist assessment base
4.   cultural stereotyping

Briefly, these problems can be recognised as follows:

1. Colour blindness

This is a common problem which is still widespread in many areas. It happens when white staff have real difficulties in "seeing" a black person and will say that "there are not many coloured people in this area" or "we treat them all the same - they are just children to us" or "her mother is white and we prefer to think of her in that way" or "she's not really black, she's Chinese/ brown/ Indian". White workers can feel even safer in this outlook if their black colleagues or clients agree that they prefer to be regarded as white/coloured/ English. Making black children invisible in this way, for whatever reason, can lead to considerable problems for them, such increasing difficulty to feel identified with, and at home in, the black community.(17)

"The fact that you have a learning difficulty will not save you from being the victim of racism - nor will it immunise you against picking up racist attitudes." (18)

Children with disabilities, especially those who are far away from their home area in a residential establishment, often need help to make these links with other black children and adults. Many are very dependent on the awareness and willingness of individual workers to help them learn that they are black, that to be black is something to feel positive about and proud of, and to find ways to develop the strengths they will need in the future as a black adult with a disability.

2. Integration and normalisation

Colour blindness is one way in which the theory of integration can operate. It results in attempts to make black children and adults fit into service provision which was designed for white people. The principle is one which therefore ignores or devalues people with black skin and black minority ethnic cultures. For black children with

disabilities, this problem is compounded by the inaccurate and damaging application of the concept of *"normalisation"*, which was developed by Bengt Nirje in the 1960s. He defined it as follows: *"The normalisation principle means making available to all mentally retarded people patterns of life and conditions of everyday living, which are as close as possible to the regular circumstances and ways of life of society"* (19)

Since then a number of misconceptions about the principle have developed. Nirje stressed that the principle is based on respect for others, the acceptance of those with disabilities with their disability, and offering them the same rights and opportunities as are available to others, with all that implies in terms of responsibility, freedom of choice and exercising personal preferences.

What he did not mean by it was that those with disabilities should be required to conform to values and life styles chosen by others; nor that they should never receive specialist services; nor be expected to function in the community without support. The dangers in such a misinterpretation for black children are apparent; already in a society which demands conformity to a Eurocentric norm, they are also liable to unnecessary and unfair pressures to compare themselves or be compared to "normal people" and then try to fit themselves into such a mould.

Sch.2(6), which gives local authorities the duty to provide services designed-

"(a) to minimise the effect on disabled children within their area of their disabilities; and
(b) to give such children the opportunity to lead lives which are as normal as possible."

is liable to such misinterpretation, and needs special care when being used in the assessment of black and minority ethnic children.

3
Chapter

Social Work Agencies & Families

3. Racist assessment base

Connections are now being made between the practice of normalisation and racism, which has led some organisations and projects to understand how inappropriate their assessments were, and therefore how inaccurate and invalid their conclusions.

" *Understandably, the professionals' joint decision has to be taken into account when deciding which school would be suitable for the child, but the parents' presence (at assessment conferences) could surely only help in providing vital information where there are gaps, such as when the child, being in a strange environment, has not 'performed' as he normally would in his home environment. The fact that the unit employs all-white professionals can be very upsetting for a child.." (20)*

For good practice ideas which can be adapted to suit children with different types of disabilities, see Double Discrimination which includes a great deal of information about schemes around the country.

4. Cultural stereotyping

In situations where efforts have been made to take into account a black child's ethnicity and cultural background, there are still many examples of stereotyping. Perhaps the most common is the assumption that black children have large kinship networks which are supportive, and that therefore many social services are not needed. Whilst this may be the case more than in many white families, there are also many black families who are extremely isolated. This may be due to migration and separation by long distance; differences of attitude and lifestyle as new generations move on; issues about the child's disability; or practical problems about staying in touch due to money or health problems.

TEAM EXERCISE

return to the exercise on p.50
(assessment of "normal" lives)

Did you decide that you would do a different assessment for black children and white children?
Would you now make any changes to that decision?

how are your agency's anti-racism and other equal opportunities policies carried out in respect of children with disabilities? :

a) is there a policy?

b) is it translated into practice by, for example:

* the appointment of staff from black and minority ethnic groups;

* finding black foster carers for black children with disabilities;

* anti-racist and anti-sexist educational and play material in nurseries and residential establishments;

* the involvement of minority ethnic advisers in reviews and conferences;

* positive encouragement to black young people to make links with the black community in the area in which they will live as adults;

* resources - money, time, premises and so on - made available for self help groups.

If your team does not have this information, try breaking down the task into a fact finding exercise, where everyone has one or two things to discover before the next meeting.

* Contact a local self-help group, or arrange a meeting with black carers. Find out what their priorities are for services from your agency; how they see their role in relation to you and what kind and quality of service they expect.

What are the connections between anti-racist and anti-discriminatory work with children with disabilities, and the duties and provisions in the Children Act?

1.   *Provide services which are designed to promote children's upbringing within their families*

* complements the purpose of the welfare duty s.17

2.   *Make an accurate assessment of children's identities, needs, abilities and supports, leading to the appropriate provision of services*

* fulfils the duty to provide appropriate services, s.17

* has regard to the racial origin of children in need, sch.2(11)

* has regard to the child's racial origin, religious persuasion, cultural and linguistic background, s.22(5)

* enables professionals to decide whether children are of sufficient understanding to take steps to which they are entitled, ss.4, 10, 43, 44

3.   *Consult children adequately*

* fulfils the duties under ss.1, 20, 22

4.   *Involve families in decision making about their children and acknowledge their expertise*

* underpins the principle of working in partnership with parents, and the assumption that children are best cared for within the family

* fulfils the duties to consult parents and other involved adults, s.22

* is compatible with the concept of ongoing and shared parental responsibility, s.2

5.   *Include families as fully as possible in assessments, in order that the needs of other family members are not overlooked*

* supports working in partnership

* suitable services for family members will be provided, s.17

6. *Provide information to parents and other carers and be prepared to receive information from them . Make this relevant and accessible, and available in as many different ways as possible to avoid ignorance and misunderstanding*

*fulfils the duties to publicise services and representations and complaints procedures in a way which makes that information accessible to those who may need them, sch.2, ss.19, 26.

VII.   ASSESSMENT WORK WITH BLACK CHILDREN AND THEIR FAMILIES

The Children Act makes a unique contribution to the development of child care law and practice in this country, by its acknowledgement that children's race, culture, religion and language should be given consideration when making certain decisions about them. The duties that it lays on local authorities and others as a consequence apply to all children, - white and black - from all families and backgrounds. The reason for including these duties is not, however, because white English children have, on the whole, experienced discrimination as a result of these elements of their lives being ignored or ridiculed. They are included because black and minority ethnic children have suffered this discrimination, and because it is known to be so widespread that an overall principle had to be introduced and influence exerted to improve practice nationally. Included in this group for instance are Irish and Jewish children, who have also suffered considerable discrimination or religious hatred.

How far do the new duties and powers enable or demand that practitioners change the traditions and attitudes which are ingrained in their agency's and their own ways of working? In this section, we will look at how they may be interpreted and propose some ideas for positive action.

The basis for anti- racist assessment work

The Children Act, as a whole piece of legislation, applies to all children in England and Wales, regardless of their skin colour, nationality, legal status, class, physical and mental abilities and so on. Black and white children are, technically, all protected from harm or neglect by the provisions in Parts III, IV and V, and are all entitled to services, if they qualify as children in need, under Part III. Unfortunately, for many black children, this is as far as equality goes. We know that black children and their families receive fewer welfare services and experience greater social control than their white counterparts.(21) In this context, practitioners using any part of the legislation, when working with any child from any family, will need to establish the principle to which they are working. This is because anti-racist policies do not come into their own simply when assessing black children. They will inform every assessment, intervention and provision of service, even for white social workers who work exclusively with white families.

The reason for this is because:

*   no assessment work is ever neutral;
(see beginning of Chapter 3)

*   to take no action against racism, in whatever context, effectively condones it *

*   our systems and agencies are based on racist thinking and practices; and

*   anti-racist practice is entirely different from being "ethnically sensitive," being "aware of the cultural issues," or even "giving due consideration to racial origin, religious persuasion, cultural and linguistic background". It assumes a level of awareness, an understanding of how racism operates in wider society, within and between agencies, structures and procedures and, on an individual level, between worker and family.

Taking personal responsibility

Some practitioners lack confidence in their own knowledge and understanding of racism and of anti-racist practice, and this can inhibit their ability to do anything about it. Both black and white workers can be affected. Although all black staff will have experienced racism at some time or another, they have much in common with white staff who are isolated, vulnerable in terms of future job security or promotion prospects, have had little opportunity to discuss the practical effects of racism on their clients, and so on. Here are some suggestions which may help to focus your thinking and plans; try to add some more of your own.

All workers

* What is your own definition of racism? What makes this definition true for you? (This may result from, for example, personal experience, reading or political analysis.)

Black workers

* How do you experience racism in your workplace? Have you been able to discuss this with anyone? What kind of supports would you need to be able to challenge racism in the future? (For example: clearer policies to rely on, training for colleagues, a commitment by others to challenge too.)

White workers

* Thinking of your past practice, how do you now understand that you were racist in your attitudes or behaviour towards colleagues or clients? Try to be as specific as possible, and ask a friend or colleague to talk with you about your beliefs and experiences. (This can be hard to admit and to explore; it may be helpful if your friend would like to do the same exercise herself/himself.) Are there differences in your current practice? What has caused this change? What do you think you still need to work on?

All workers

* What are your strengths in working against racism? Who can help you to overcome them and how can you go about getting that help?

Acknowledging your organisation's position on race

If we work from a basis which acknowledges that:

* British society is racist,

* organisational racism is an integral and powerful influence in social work,

* social work policies reflect that racism, as do

* social work theories, methods and attitudes

then we can begin to understand the extent to which practitioners must challenge themselves and the constructs of their practice when working with black families. Many do this already; many are supported by committed management and elected members determined to eradicate its racist behaviour; others work in isolation and under great stress.

- How is your agency racist, in its:

(a)   policies, or lack of them. Try reading through your child care policy document or child protection procedures for positive statements about black and minority ethnic families.

(b)   its systems and procedures. These may actively exclude or unintentionally marginalise black staff and clients by, for example failing to listen to specialist advisers, exploiting staff by insisting that they act as intepreters, and failure to make information available to clients in their own language.

(c)   its practice. This can vary enormously, and can include failing to acknowledge that black people live in your area, or to challenge racist statements by white staff or clients, and not paying attention to the needs of black children being looked after to develop a strong black identity.

Chapter 3

Social Work Agencies & Families

*   What are you reading which will help you to develop your thinking, both about the experiences of different black people in Britain, and about anti-racist practice? There are many books and articles now available

*   What do you really know about who lives in your area? (See the exercise: Know your community on p. 26) Try applying this to your own work. For example: if you are in fostering or day care, do you know the proportion of under 8s in the different ethnic communities (including white British)? How does this information connect to decisions about recruitment of staff and carers, knowledge about cultural differences, language and so on?

*   Think of a particular piece of work you have done, which you think you could have done differently if you had known more about the ethnicity or culture of the family, or about anti-racist work. What specifically could have helped you in that situation, and what would you like to have done differently? It may be helpful to talk to your team leader or colleagues about arranging these supports or information for the future.

The duties and powers in the Children Act

(i)   We have already mentioned above (p72) that all children are covered by all parts of the Act. When a black child is assessed as being in need, the welfare duty applies:

" It shall be the general duty of every local authority... -

a)   to safeguard and promote the welfare of children within their area who are in need..." s. 17(1)

No child's welfare can be adequately addressed without attention to her or his race, culture, language and religion. In order to meet their obligations under this Part, therefore, social work practice must always be anti-racist and anti-discriminatory. Without this starting point, black children's welfare may not be safeguarded, and certainly will not be promoted. Workers may need to overcome inhibitions about asking all children and families about their background, and find ways to do this which makes sense to both clients and themselves. Many people are deeply anxious and suspicious about divulging personal details, for good reasons, in a climate of changing racial and religious hatreds, and this must always be respected. Others will not see the point when they are requesting a service such as childminding or aids and adaptations.

CHECKPOINT

*   When did you last ask a child or family for information about their race, culture, religion or language? Did you feel at ease? If not, try to work out what the problem was, and practice asking a colleague in a different way.

(ii)   When a local authority is arranging day care and fostering services, they will in future be bound by this duty:

" Every local authority shall, in making any arrangements -

a)   for the provision of day care within their area; or

b)   designed to encourage persons to act as local authority foster parents, have regard to the different racial groups to which children within their area who are in need belong." sch.2,11

A minimalist response to this would be for authorities simply to ask the parents of all children requiring these services their racial origin, as and when they apply for them.

An anti-racist response would include comprehensive ethnic monitoring of:

(a) the community as a whole;

(b) the under 8s in different ethnic groups;

(c) all children currently receiving day care or foster care;

(d) all staff and carers currently employed; and

(e) a review of current service provision and the allocation of resources in light of the above, paying particular attention to:

* the type of provision available and its appropriateness for the families you have identified;

* the recruitment of appropriate staff and carers;

* policies operating regarding same race placements, and resource allocated to make this work viable;

* the effectiveness of policies in nurseries and with regard to childminders;

* training, guidance and support given to carers to enable them to provide anti-racist care;

* resources to ensure that this can be carried out and supported by, for example:

- the inclusion of a senior manager, and the support of elected members,

- allocation of additional administrative staff,

- negotiation with unions about levels of unacceptable bevaviour and sanctions, including dismissal,

- time made available for staff to receive training or advice as necessary.

(iii) A new duty which is closely linked to the above is:

" A local authority may at any time cancel the registration of any person under section 71(1)(a) if

...b) the care provided by that person when looking after any child as a child minder is, in the opinion of the authority, seriously inadequate having regard to the needs of that child; s.74(1)

" In considering the needs of any child for the purposes of subsection (1)(b) or (2)(b), a local authority shall, in particular, have regard to the child's religious persuasion, racial origin and cultural and linguistic background." s.74,(6)

This duty will be welcomed by many local authority staff who have been looking for stronger powers in relation to racist behaviour by childminders or nursery staff. It is a pity that the wording of the Act does not encourage a proactive role by insisting that adequate care **shall** be provided for children in this way, instead of allowing the authority not to act until a serious situation has developed. However, this does not prevent an authority from taking this step themselves.

Chapter 3

Social Work Agencies & Families

A positive anti-racist response might include the following:

* Ask service users and providers to tell you how they think you could have regard to their race, culture, religion and language. This should include all aspects of your assessment work, provision of the day care, reviews of the minder or nursery. What examples can they give you of what they would consider "seriously inadequate" care?

* Find out who has been doing some work in this area already. For example, the Commission for Racial Equality produced a very useful booklet, "From cradle to school" (22) which incorporates practical ideas and other resources.

* Provide training for day care officers and others who will be responsible for monitoring standards. This new role will involve these workers in much more direct contact at the negotiating stage between parents and minders; it may be helpful for them to talk to fostering workers who have already incorporated anti-racist policies into their practice.

* Draw up criteria for what is to be considered good, adequate, inadequate and seriously inadequate care. Without having done this, it will be very hard to deal properly with complaints, to impose further requirements on carers, to offer appropriate training or to de-register in the final stages.

(iv) In Chapter 4, we look in detail at the duties to have regard to race, culture, religion and language when looking after children, and suggest that a similar process could be useful for day care services also. These state:

"In making any such decision (ie. with respect to a child they are looking after or proposing to look after) a local authority shall give due consideration :

...c) to the child's religious persuasion, racial origin and cultural and linguistic background" s. 22(5)

ASSESSING THE FAMILIES OF BLACK CHILDREN

In all of the situations outlined above, that is, the provision of services under Part III and Schedule 2 of the Act, and when working with families with a view to initiating or intervening in court proceedings, social workers will undertake some form of assessment work with the black child's family. In some situations, the contact will be minimal, such as a one-off request for emergency cash help due to non-payment of a benefit cheque; in others, there will be extensive and detailed work.

The assessment checklist on page 81 will of course be valid in work with both black and white families, but two, crucial, added dimensions for any black family will be:
(a) their own experience of racism and its effect on the assessment situation and interaction, and
(b) the personal and institutional stance of the worker and agency on anti-racism.
We noted in Chapter 1 that a conference organised by the REU and LBTC in 1990, "Working with the strengths of black families" (23) had studied the different results which can ensue from approaching this work from two different models: deficit or empowerment. The first relies on a problem-orientated framework of practice, which emphasises the control and authority of the worker. Families are regarded as having "deficits" or as being in some way "dysfunctional". The damage which may be caused by an over-reliance on negative criteria can be compounded for black families due to the ignorance, assumptions and lack of awareness displayed by social workers towards them. The contrast between this approach and one which is based on the strengths, abilities and positive contribution which a family can make to their life, including overcoming obstacles, was highlighted by a small group led by Ratna Dutt. The group's conclusions are noted below.

The group worked on a case study about a single black woman with a child, who had herself been in care, now returning to work and requiring day care. The group explored, first of all, the "deficit" model, and listed the following characteristics of such an approach, together with the information which would "confirm" the theory. They then contrasted the theory and practice outcomes with working from a model of "empowerment".

1. Deficit model

i)	pathological assumption	aggressive, abusive
ii)	cultural stereotypes	single parent=bad parent institutional care=bad parent
iii)	blaming the victim	single parent=inability to cope return to work=uncaring parent
iv)	professional superiority	we know best
v)	knowledge base of social work	institutional care= inadequate parents family nuclear model best
vi)	power relationship	inherent imbalance between parent and nursery staff
vii)	cultural superiority	black parents can't cope because large numbers black children in care
viii)	racism	whole process
ix)	social work action	worst - removal of child

2. Empowerment model

i)	recognition of life experience	surviving care, racist system, as single parent
ii)	understanding black experience	learned hard way about being black in white society
iii)	sensitivity to cultural pride	good mother - self referral, proved can get job
iv)	positive self image	assertive re child's needs, can get job
v)	knowledge of family/support system	holistic approach
vi)	role model	for black children in care - they can get jobs, survive
vii)	redress power imbalance	work in partnership with parent, break down them and us divisions
viii)	work against racism	stop stereotyping, use positive images, accept different norms as different, not inferior, acknowledge worker's power base
ix)	social worker's action	examine whole culture of organisation, reviews and complaints procedures.

Chapter 3

*Social Work
Agencies
& Families*

Child protection assessments perhaps pinpoint most clearly the absolute necessity of having a well developed body of knowledge and practice on anti-racism. A recent development in social work has been to become "culturally informed" about "different" minority ethnic groups. This is characterised by a view held by white workers that they must learn all there is to know (if such a thing were possible) about the customs and cultures of their clients, in order to make accurate assessments. Whilst this knowledge is of course essential, it pre-empts the first stage, which is to understand that the whole situation, including the assessment, arises within a system of values and beliefs which generally and specifically denigrates and dis-empowers black people.

This knowledge is carried by both worker and family, at different levels. The worker must acknowledge this fact and reflect the knowledge in her or his practice. This may happen in a number of ways. Some of them will concern cultural assumptions; for example the over-generalisation about the strength and capacity of Caribbean grandmothers; the significance of the adult/child bond; the relevance of non-related adults. Other ways will be to challenge other professionals who make racist statements; challenging one's own agency policies in respect of black families; empowering black communities to be able to understand and fully participate in the assessment.

A fuller discussion of the whole issue can be found in "Towards a black perspective in child protection" by Phillips and Dutt (24).

RACE CULTURE, RELIGION AND LANGUAGE

Anti-racist services to all members of the community

are based on

constant personal evaluation of attitudes and practice

which is supported by

team learning together

in the context of

local office culture geared to anti-discriminatory practice

which depends on

interaction with local community

and

**anti-discriminatory recruitment and staffing practice;
ethnic monitoring of staff and services;
well established reviewing procedures**

which are reflected in

positive equality statements in departmental child care policy document, child protection procedures and complaints procedures

to which

senior manager and elected members are committed

and are supported by

**The Children Act 1989
sections 17(1) 22(5) 74(6) Sch 2(II)
and
The Race Relations Act 1976
sections 20 and 71**

VIII. ASSESSMENT - CHILDREN SUFFERING OR LIKELY TO SUFFER HARM

the care of a reasonable parent

Parts IV and V of the Act cover those situations in which social workers and others have to make assessments and decisions about the extent to which children may be suffering harm and how far this is attributable to the care they are receiving from their parents.

Children can now only be admitted to care by a single route,care proceedings, and the grounds which must be satisfied are as follows:

"(a)   that the child is suffering, or is likely to suffer, significant harm; and

(b)   that the harm, or likelihood of harm, is attributable to-

    (i)   the care given to the child, or likely to be given to him if the order were not made, not being what it would be reasonable to expect a parent to give to him; or

    (ii)   the child's being beyond parental control".s.31

Here the concept of the hypothetical parent being a reasonable parent is introduced, and controversy about its interpretation will be the subject of much courtroom debate in the next few years. The D.o.H. is clear that the question should not revolve around whether the particular parent in question is reasonable, given their circumstances and characteristics, but on what the court considers a parent would consider reasonable and judge the parent according to the objective criteria: what care would a reasonable parent give to the particular child before the court?

Social workers will have to make these judgements themselves in order to bring their cases to court, and so we will be looking here at what is acceptable, reasonable, good-enough care, and at how far such generalities can be applied objectively.

TRUE OR FALSE?
or
WHERE IS THE REASONABLE PARENT?

1.   A reasonable parent never hits their child in anger.

2.   A reasonable parent provides for their child at every level - physical, emotional, material, etc.

3.   Married couples are intrinsically better at parenting than non-married couples.

4.   A reasonable father provides as much care as a reasonable mother.

5.   A reasonable parent will always provide a higher standard of care for a child with disabilities.

6.   Grandparents are often better at parenting than parents are.

7.   It is impossible to be a reasonable parent all the time.

I guess that everyone is in agreement about that last one!

Although it is not always overtly stated in social work policies and texts, our professional definitions and assumptions about where to locate reasonable parenting are firmly fixed in white, middle class nuclear families. In some of our more influential guidance, such as the D.oH. 'orange book' on assessment (25), the model is explicitly provided. Take for example, the Family Life Cycle on page 82:

1.   The unattached young adult
2.   The newly married couple
3.   The family with young children
4.   The family with adolescents
5.   Launching children and moving on
6.   The family in later life

In some ways this is very familiar; many people in Britain will separate from their parents as young adults, many will marry,

Chapter 3

*Social Work
Agencies
& Families*

will have children, will see their children grow and will themselves grow into old age. However, the majority will also experience a number of ways in which this model does not hold true, for themselves, their close relatives and friends. The existence of such a model and its partner 'dislocation of the family cycle' which only covers divorce, clearly implies that families which do not fit it are somehow 'dislocated' or dysfunctional.

What message does this hold for anyone who is not married or is divorced with children; for the parents of the 360,000 children with disabilities, some of whom may never be able to live independently; to the 10% of the population who are lesbian and gay, and for whom the concept of "real" family life is denied; for those who are too poor for their young adults to leave home; for the millions who have been raised by a number of relatives and friends, and are themselves part of a network of caring adults; for those in care for whom leaving home means saying goodbye to your social worker?

To all these people and many more it says 'This is not for you, you don't fit, and you are by implication less acceptable as a model of reasonable parenting.'

TEAM EXERCISE

(with facilitator - this exercise requires trust between team members, and willingness to discuss personal views and experiences.)

1. Everyone to anonymously write down on separate pieces of paper, 3 examples of family life, briefly giving information about numbers of adults and children, legal and significant relationships between them:

　　- your own　　　　　　　　- a friend's　　　　　　　　- a client's.

2. Put them all together and mix them up. Take it in turns to read out an example. Find out how many fit into the Family Life Cycle described and order them accordingly. Discuss what are the characteristics which for you identify a family and compare them with this model.

3. Discuss in which of these families a child might receive 'reasonable parenting'. What are the characteristics which influence your judgement?

4. For some workers, it will be impossible to do this exercise either because they can't trust their colleagues enough to tell them about their family, and fear identification by taking part, or to say what they really feel about acceptable lifestyles.

　　If this is the case, ask your facilitator to guide you in a less difficult exercise on your views about parenting. You may still identify obstacles in the process of setting up the exercise and specific training may be needed before you can start.

5. Finally, discuss what position this leaves your clients in, when working with you about their children. You can measure this by the ease or difficulty with which you and your team were able to undertake the exercise. Were you nervous, angry, alienated, relieved, bored? Did you try to focus attention on to someone else so that you would be left alone? Did you strongly disapprove of someone else's lifestyle and find it impossible to say so; or experience that disapproval?

When you visit families to assess their abilities to parent a child or children, they will inevitably feel some of these powerful emotions in addition to the knowledge that:

(a) something is wrong for you to be involved;

(b) you have told them nothing about yourself;

(c) you have something you are measuring them by;

(d) you have the power to judge them, and remove their children if necessary.

I. ASSESSMENT CHECKLIST

I THE FAMILY IN A WIDER CONTEXT

1. *The family in a wider society.*
What is the combination of factors which make up this particular family's identity and affects their position within society as a whole? (include e.g. ethnicity, class, culture, language, employment and housing status, health, sexuality and disability)

2. *The family in the local community.*
How is the local community comprised? What are the facilities and services which affect the whole family's self-image, identity and abilities?

3. *The family and racism.*
What are the actual or potential effects of racism on this family? (Examples include: personal experiences of physical and verbal violence; previous dealings with racist institutions and officials; fears about immigration status)

4. *The family and the development of strengths.*
What are the particular strengths which this family has developed as a result of dealing with hardships such as poverty, chronic ill-health or racism?

5. *The experience of individual family members.*
What are the differing effects on individuals within this family of the factors identified in 1.? (For example: do they share the same religious belief? What is the effect of this on shared family values, attitudes, lifestyles and daily routines? If they have suffered a particular hardship, such as long-term unemployment, how has this been felt by different family members?

II THE FAMILY AND THE SOCIAL WORK AGENCY

6. *The effect of the social work agency on assessment.*
What is the direct effect on your work of the agency you represent? How does this family view your agency as a whole -helpful, intrusive? What is the effect of institutional racism (whether intentional or unintentional, by yours or another agency) on the relationship between you and the family?

III THE FAMILY'S ASSESSMENT

7. *The family's view.*
How does the family (different family members) see their strengths, characteristics, abilities, needs and problems?

8. *The immediate problem.*
How does the family define the problem for which they are seeking help/ about which they have been referred to you?

9. *The child and family.*
Does the family think the child is in need, and if so, why? On what have they based their views and how do they see a resolution? Who do they think can help, in what way, for how long; what do they see as the pros and cons of different possibilities?

IV   THE CHILD IN THE FAMILY

10.   ***What is the position of this child in relation to the rest of the family,*** in respect of the characteristics already identified in 1,4 and 5? (Examples include: the only member of the family with severe hearing impairment; a young person with a different religion; the role expectation of the oldest girl.)

11.   *The child's view.*

'   Does the child think that she or he is in need and if so, why? In what way? Does the child's view differ from that of other family members?

V   THE FAMILY AND THE WORKER

12.   *The effect of the worker's identity.*

What factors do you bring to the work which affect the assessment which results? (see introduction to the chapter: authority, purpose, principles, identity,"baggage"); in particular, what is the effect of your age, gender and ethnicity on your relationship with different family members?

13.   *Definition of family.*

How do you define "family"? Does this vary from one assessment situation to another, and if so, why and how? Does your definition differ from the family's and if so, how and what difference does it make (it will make a difference). Who do you routinely include in your assessment? Who do you routinely exclude? Who do you consciously ask about if they are not around or referred to? Do you routinely include non-blood relatives, such as godparents and close friends? Do you assess the contribution of these people differently, and if so, how?

14.   *Acceptable families.*

Do you believe that some families or lifestyles are less valid or acceptable than others? If so, why and in which ways? What differences does this make to your assessment? How do you inform the family and note the influence of your views? (Examples may be of single parents, poor families with many children, gay fathers, travelling families.)

15.   *Worker's lack of knowledge.*

What is the effect on this assessment of your lack of information, experience or understanding in some areas? (Examples include: the physical and mental effects of particular disabilities or illnesses; the influence of migrating from one country to another on family lifestyle, health, economics and so on.) How do you acknowledge your lack of knowledge to the family and note the influence on the assessment?

X.   FAMILY NEEDS ASSESSMENT AND PLAN

(a suggested model)

1.   *Routine Information*

A.   **Family life.**
     Who lives at home?   Ages   Relationships
     Who lives away from home?   Ages   Relationships
     Note who is a parent and who has parental responsibility

B.   **Important others:**
     Relationships   Addresses/tel nos.

C.   **What is your family's ethnic background?**
     Note different ethnic origin of family members as necessary
     Which language is most often spoken/written by your family? Other languages.

D.   **What is your family's cultural background?**
     This includes e.g.class, standards of living, kinds of work and education, the kind
     of leisure activities you enjoy, how you raise your children, attitudes towards older
     people in the family, relationships between men and women in the family, and
     between parents and adolescents.

E.   **Religious background and current beliefs:**
     Note effect on attitudes, behaviour, daily routines, conflicting beliefs amongst
     family members.

F.   **Employment; benefits; education/training:**
     Note attitudes and effects of unemployment or different family members.

G.   **Income/ expenses**
     Note sources and amount of income and regular/irregular expenses

H.   **Background information**
     Note any previous important relationships, jobs, housing moves, obstacles
     overcome.

2.   *Describe how your child's health or development is being "significantly
impaired" (seriously affected or damaged).*

        If more than one child is affected, describe them separately.

3.   *In what specific ways does your child's difficulty, disability or need affect
other people in the family?*

4. *Type and levels of support your child and/or family require:*

a) Is your total family income enough to meet your child's medical, child care and other related expenses?

b) Is your accommodation adequate to meet your child's needs?

c) Do you receive any social or medical services for your child, e.g. day care, occupational therapy?

d) Do you belong to any voluntary organisation which gives you advice or support with your child's needs?

e) Do you get any helpful information from e.g. the library, clinic?

f) Do you see a counsellor?

g) Do you regularly visit a clinic or doctor for your child?

h) Do you use respite care for your child?

i) Has your child spent any time in foster or residential care?

j) Does your child have regular daycare at a nursery, playgroup or with a childminder, or from the education department?

k) **Do you get the support you need from:**

family	friends
other parents	your other children
colleagues at work	professionals, e.g. teacher, health visitor
your religion/place of worship	recreational activities

any other....

l) What additional support, training, services, equipment, etc. do you need to care for your child at home and why?

Refer to the list: *Explanation*

Child care
Counselling (e.g. marital, drug abuse, genetic)
Advocacy/advice (e.g. debts, housing benefits or about other forms of complaints)
Respite care
Parentcraft course
More informal support
Translated information
Transport, including vehicle modification
Occupational, speech or behaviour therapy
Architectural modifications
Home help
Special clothing or diet
Literacy class
Recreational facilities
Assertiveness training
Any other

m) What does your family need the most, and is not receiving?

n) You may be charged for some of the services listed above, unless you receive income support or family credit. Are you willing to have a means test (i.e. fill in a form about your income and expenses) to find out if you can get help towards the cost?

(If you are charged for services and don't pay, you may be taken to court).

CHAPTER THREE REFERENCES

1. as above, Chapter 1 no.5

2. as above, Chapter 1 no.5

3. Population Trends no.60 p.37; p.35
OPCS   Summer 1990

4. as above, Chapter 1 no.5

5. as above, Chapter 1 no.6

6. as above, Chapter 1 no.9

7. Child care policy:
putting it in writing
SSI, HMSO   1990

8. The care of children:
principles and practice in regulations
and guidance
DoH, HMSO 1990

9. Rocking the cradle:
Lesbian mother, a challenge in the
family
G. Hanscombe & J. Forster

10. as above, no.8

11. Social work decisions in child care
D.H.S.S. H.M.S.O 1985

12. as above, no.8

13. Community Care Magazine 1990

14. Protecting children.
A guide for social workers
undertaking a comprehensive
assessment
DoH, HMSO   1988

15. Language and Power journal no.197

16. Physical and mental handicap in
the Asian community.
Can my child be helped?
H.Davis and P.Russell, NCB 1989

17. Colour blindness
J.Cheetham in New Society 26/8/87

18. as above, Chapter 1 no.16

19. Setting the record straight:
a critique of some frequent
misconceptions of the normalization
principle
B.Perrin and B.Nirje in Australia and
New Zealand Journal of
Developmental Disabilities 1985
Vol.11 no.2 69-74

20. as above, Chapter 1 no.34

21. as above, Chapter 1 no.15

22. From cradle to school
CRE 1989

23. as above, Chapter 1 no.33

24. Towards a black perspective in child
protection
M.Phillips and R.Dutt, REU 1990

25. as above no.12

FURTHER READING SUGGESTIONS

1. Framework for the future -
promoting race equality and valued
social roles for people with learning
difficulties
P.Ferns, K.Kurowski, L.Colledge and
P.Wakeford co-ordinated by LBTC/
published CCETSW - forthcoming

2. Defining and assessing black
families
S.Ahmed in Planning for children,
FRG 1988

3. The Children Act 1989 -
What's in it for grandparents
F.R.G. / Grandparents Federation
1991

PRINCIPLES OF THE ACT

Children's welfare is the court's paramount consideration	Children are to be consulted regarding all decisions to be made about them, and must be given information about the Act's provisions.	Children may take action to initiate, prevent or complain about certain matters.	Children have the right to protection from harm and neglect.	Children are to be helped to live with their families and to stay in touch with them.

LOCAL AUTHORITIES' DUTIES AND POWERS TOWARDS CHILDREN WHO ARE LOOKED AFTER

Consider children's race, culture, religion, language. s.22	Consult children and those important to them. ss.1,22,26	Provide accommodation suited to the needs of children with disabilities. s.23 NO	Arrange for children to live with family or friends or promote and sustain contact between them. s.23 , Sch.2(10)(15)	Prepare children and young people for moving on, and support them into independence. S.24

PRINCIPLES AND PRACTICE GUIDE

No.12	No.15	No.19	No.26
Parents should be expected and enabled to retain their responsibilities and to remain as closely involved as is consistent with their child's welfare, even if that child cannot live at home either temporarily or permanently.	Wider families matter as well as parents -especially siblings and grandparents.	Every young person needs to develop a secure sense of personal identity.	As young people grow up, preparation for independence is a necessary and important part of the parental role which child care agencies carry for young people in long-term care.

EQUALITY ISSUES

Actively promoting rights of children with disabilities to highest quality child care services.	Initiating anti-discriminatory policies in residential work, family centres, fostering and adoption teams.	Recognising the necessity for consistent anti-racist practice in all settings.	Developing ideas for working in partnership with children and young people.

CHAPTER FOUR
SOCIAL WORK AGENCIES AND CHILDREN

I.   THE ACT'S FRAMEWORK AND CONTEXT

1. Terminology

There are several new pieces of terminology which need to be understood in order to be clear about the status of children and about the duties of local authorities and others towards them (see below, page 91). Amongst the most important are:

*   children who are "looked after" by a local authority

*   children in "accommodation" provided by the local authority

*   children who are "in care".

i)   children who are looked after are defined in s.22 (1) as:
"in their care; or provided with accommodation by the authority ...."

and "...'accommodation' means accommodation which is provided for a continuous period of more than 24hours." (s.22(2))

ii)   a child for whom local authorities must provide this accommodation is defined in s.20(1), as one in need who appears to need it as a result of:

"(a) there being no person who has parental responsibility for him;

 (b) his being lost or abandoned; or

(c) the person who has been caring for him being prevented (whether or not permanently, and for whatever reason) from providing him with suitable accommodation or care."

Local authorities may also provide accommodation where someone with parental responsibility could care for the child, if this would safeguard or promote the child's welfare (s.20(4)). This enables them to provide, for example, respite accommodation for any child.

Provision must also be made for 16 and 17 year olds in need "whose welfare the authority consider is likely to be seriously prejudiced if they do not provide him with accommodation"(s.22 (3))

It is envisaged that, in most circumstances, arrangements for the accommodation will be made on a negotiated and voluntary basis between agency and family. This is consistent with the position regarding parental responsibility and working in partnership. (see below)

iii)   Children will only be in care if they have been the subject of a successful application under s.31 of the Act. This single route replaces the various options previously available, such as through wardship, matrimonial care orders and criminal proceedings. The concept of voluntary care disappears altogether.

2. Working in partnership - a new impetus

This is one of the key principles of the Children Act, but the words themselves do not appear anywhere in the legislation. In many ways the principle is implicit, both in providing services and in court proceedings.

Partnership and parental responsibility are, for instance, closely aligned. The concept and application of parental responsibility are discussed in Chapter 3, page 50 .

The important points to note in this context are that there are crucial differences between children in care and those provided with accommodation in respect of who has parental responsibility for them. (see chart on page). With the latter group, the authority does not acquire parental responsibility, but it remains with the parents or whoever had it under a court order. However, when children are in care, the authority shares it with the parents (including a non-married father if he has a s.4 agreement or order). Although there are restrictions on the extent to which the authority may exert that responsibility (for example they cannot change a child's name or consent to adoption, s.33(6)&(7)), they may restrict the way in which the parents exercise their parental responsibility if they believe it is necessary to do so in order to safeguard or promote the child's welfare (s.33(3)&(4)).

3. The role of the court

In care proceedings, courts will have much wider areas of consideration (section 1 duties) and greater powers regarding flexible orders and directions, such as the ability to make section 8 orders or orders about contact. More people will have access to court proceedings generally (for example, those with parental responsibility and children requesting section 8 orders). By legislating that parental responsibility is to be shared between parents or guardians and the local authority after the making of a care order, the Act establishes clearly that an active partnership between all those involved with children should be encouraged and sustained throughout their upbringing. In particular, the application of the "presumption of no order" concept in s.1(5) will put pressure on social workers to come to court with evidence that they have already started to make plans and agreements with family members, and that the order will be a useful part of that plan. There are of course provisions for restricting this if it is necessary to safeguard a child, but Principle 12 should form the basis on which the work is established. (see chart p.86)

4. Contact

This principle of active partnership is supported by the new duties regarding contact between children being looked after and their families. This must be promoted for all children who are looked after and reasonable contact must be arranged for children on care orders. Arrangements for this latter group can be further defined and strengthened by a court order under section 34. The Act makes clearer the principle that contact is beneficial to children and that such arrangements are being made for their benefit rather than the adults involved, whether they be parent, foster carer, social worker, or agency.

The Principles and Practice Guide, nos.14-16, and the duties in sch.2(15) also lay considerable emphasis on promoting and sustaining links between children and their wider family networks and communities. This emphasis arises out of the bitter experience of many young people who, having left care, have voiced their anger and grief at having lost contact with all those who were once significant in their lives, and not had them replaced with any satisfactory long term alternative. The long- term effects of either deliberate or unintentional severing of links have been to leave many young people particularly isolated, unable to relate to their own communities, with great damage having been done to their sense of identity and self-esteem. This is especially true for black young people for whom the racism they experienced in care has hurt and angered them, and left them acutely aware that the system has not equipped them to take their place as confident, resourceful citizens within a racist society.

5. Children accommodated elsewhere

Thousands of children in Britain live away from home, either temporarily or permanently, in establishments run by voluntary organisations, health and education departments. Many children are also privately fostered. It has been estimated that there are 127,250 children in independent boarding schools, of whom 11,300 have special needs and 5,320 have disabilities (1). For some time there has been growing concern at the lack of local authority responsibility and accountability for these children and the enormous variation in the child care services they received. Now there are new duties laid on the proprietors of establishments, on voluntary organisations and on local authorities which together provide a framework for ensuring that these children's welfare is being both safeguarded and promoted. Certain sections of the Act will be particularly relevant to them, such as the power to appoint independent visitors and to support contact arrangements:

"Where it appears to a local authority in relation to any child that they are looking after that-

communication between the child and -
(i)   a parent of his, or

(ii)   any person who is not a parent of his but who has parental responsibility for him, has been infrequent; or

he has not been visited by (or lived with) any such person during the preceding twelve months, and that it would be in the child's best interests for an independent person to be appointed to be his visitor for the purposes of this paragraph, they shall appoint such a visitor." sch.2(17)(1)

"Every local authority shall take such steps as are reasonably practicable, where any child within their area who is in need and whom they are not looking after is living apart from his family-

(a)   to enable him to live with his family; or
(b)   to promote contact between him and his family, if, in their opinion, it is necessary to do so in order to safeguard or promote his welfare." sch.2 (10)

In order for these new duties to be effective, two things are needed: good inter-agency working relationships have to be established and a large increase in resources will be required to enable the inspection duties to be carried out, together with the additional planning and service provision which will arise from those duties.

CHILDREN WHO ARE LOOKED AFTER BY THE LOCAL AUTHORITY MAY BE:-		Parental Responsibility:	
	in need Part III s.20	remains with person or persons who already have it	ALL SUCH CHILDREN WHO ARE PROVIDED WITH ACCOMMODATION FOR OVER 24 HOURS CONTINUOUSLY ARE CHILDREN "LOOKED AFTER" BY THE LOCAL AUTHORITY
	on a care order Part IV s.31	is shared between LA and parent or guardian	
	on an interim care order Part IV s. 38	is shared between LA and person who has it	
	on a child assessment order Part V s.43	remains with person who has it	
	on an emergency protection order Part V s.44	is given to applicant	
	on a police protection order Part V s.46	remains with person who has it	

II. LOCAL AUTHORITY DUTIES TOWARDS CHILDREN LOOKED AFTER BY THEM

Before accommodation is provided

1. Find out child's wishes and feelings s.20(6)

2. Find out wishes and feelings of parent, person with parental responsibility and other relevant people s.22(4)

3. Give due consideration to these wishes and feelings s.22(5)

4. Give due consideration to child's religious persuasion, racial origin and cultural and linguistic background s.22(5)(c)

5. If recruiting people to become foster carers, have regard to racial origin of children in need sch.2(11)

Making placements

1. Provide accommodation and maintain child s.23(1)

2. Place near home and keep siblings together s.23(7)

3. Place with relatives or friends unless inconsistent with welfare s.23(6)

4. Make sure accommodation 'not unsuitable' for children with disabilities s.23(8)

5. Inform parents and those with parental responsibility of whereabouts sch.2(15)

6. Consult with appropriate local education authority if providing accommodation with education s.28

7. Decide whether to charge for provision s.29

When looking after children

1. Safeguard and promote child's welfare s.22(3)(a)

2. Make use of services and facilities which would have been available to child living at home s.23(3)(b)

3. Promote contact between child, family and others connected to her or him sch.2(15)

4. Allow reasonable contact between child on care order, parents, guardians, or those previously with residence or under a s.34 court order

5. Power to pay expenses connected with promoting contact sch.2(16)

6. Power to appoint independent visitor sch.2(17)

Chapter 4

Social Work Agencies and children who are looked after

7. Duty to plan and review s.26(1)

8. Duty to set up representations and complaints procedures s.26(3)

9. Duty to inform child of her/his rights under the Act (Review of children's cases (L.A.V.O. & R.C.H. draft Reg.4(4)& Sch.I))

10. Child's ability to refuse examination and assessments s.43

11. Continue to consult as before entering accommodation s.22(4)&(5)

12. Continue to pay consideration to race, culture, language and religion s.22(5)

13. Advise, assist and befriend with a view to promoting child's welfare on leaving accommodation s.24(1)

After accommodation

1. Advise, assist and befriend certain young people, by providing assistance in kind or, exceptionally, cash s.24(1)(6)&(7)

2. Duty to inform other local authorities if young person moving to their area s.24(11)

3. Duty on other organisations to inform local authority s.24(12)

4. Proposed amendment (through Courts and Legal Services Act) : include representations procedure in s.24.

Chapter 4

Social Work
Agencies and
children who are
looked after

III CHILDREN WHO ARE PROVIDED WITH ACCOMMODATION BY OTHERS

BEFORE ACCOMMODATION PROVIDED

A. Ascertain wishes and feelings of child, parents, others
B. Give due consideration to above wishes and feelings
C. Give due consideration to religion, race, culture, language

DURING ACCOMMODATION

D. Safeguard and promote welfare
E. Make use of services and facilities available for child cared for in own family
F. Advise assist and befriend with a view to promoting welfare when no longer accommodated by them
G. Continue to ascertain wishes and feelings
H. Continue to give due consideration to race, culture, religion, language
I. Duty to notify local authority if providing accommodation for consecutive period of at least 3 month

LOCAL AUTHORITY DUTIES TOWARDS CHILDREN ACCOMMODATED ELSEWHERE

J. Check that agency or carers are safeguarding and promoting the welfare of child
K. Arrange for children in voluntary organisation accommodation to be visited and for children privately fostered to be visited
L. Where local authority not satisfied that child's welfare is satisfactorily safeguarded or promoted; duty to secure that care and accommodation of child undertaken by family and decide whether to exercise any of their functions under the Act
M. Power to enter, inspect premises and children
N. Take steps to enable child to live in family and promote contact between child and family

DUTIES / DEFINITIONS

	1 privately fostered	2 in a registered children's home	3 in voluntary home run by a voluntary organisation	4 Accommodated by a health authority	5 accommodated by an education authority	6 accommodated in residential care homes, nursing homes and mental nursing homes	7 accommodated in independent schools	8 Local Authority
A		s. 64 (2)	s. 61 (2)					
B		s. 64 (3)	s. 61 (3)					
C		s. 64 (3) (c)	s. 61 (3) (c)					
D		s. 64 (1) (a)	s. 61 (1) (a)					
E		s. 64 (1) (b)	s. 61 (1) (b)					
F		s. 64 (1) (c)	s. 61 (1) (c)					
G		s. 64 (2)	s. 61 (2)					
H		s. 64 (3)	s. 61 (3)					
I				s. 85 (1)	s. 85 (1)	s. 86(1)	s. 87 (1)	
J								s. 62 (1), s. 67 (1), s. 85 (4), s. 87 (3), s. 62 (2)
K								s. 62, s. 67
L								s. 67 (2)
M								s. 62 (6), s. 67 (3)
N								sch. 2 (10)

93

IV. MAKING ARRANGEMENTS FOR CHILDREN TO BE LOOKED AFTER

Local authorities, registered children's homes and voluntary organisations have certain duties:

* towards children for whom they are proposing to provide accommodation and

* towards children who are looked after, whatever the circumstances in which the provision of the service occurs.

Altogether, there are many of these, such as:

* children who stay regularly with a foster carer

* children who have been abandoned

* children whose carers are ill and cannot look after them

* children who are on court orders, about whom there are serious concerns for their health and welfare.

The duties are:

i) before the provision of accommodation -to consult with the child (s.20(6))

ii) when making any decision about a child they are looking after, or proposing to look after

* to consult with the child, child's parents, anyone with parental responsibility and other relevant people regarding the sion to be made and to give due consideration to their wishes and feelings (s.22(4) s.61(2)&(3) s.64(2)&(3))

* to give due consideration to the racial origin, cultural and linguistic background and religious persuasion of the child (s.22(5) s.61(3) s.64(3)).

In some situations, the agency will know little about the child or family and will have to establish a relationship with them at the point of providing the accommodation. In most cases, however, they will know each other well and matters will have been discussed with at least the child and one of the adults concerned. Consultation must take place " so far as is reasonably practicable" but race, culture, language and religion must be considered in all cases. This is one of the few unequivocal duties in the Act, and as such, should be given the highest priority when making any decision about a child who is to be looked after.

1. CONSULTATION - SETTING IT UP

Practice

To ask children and their families their feelings about the provision of accommodation is standard practice. After all, talking about feelings and exploring innermost needs, wishes and troubles is at the heart of social work. As practitioners, though, we too rarely stop to ask ourselves how our questions are being received by the person on the receiving end, in the context in which we are both trying to resolve the problem. It would be interesting to ask your clients and colleagues whether they believe that consultation is really taking place in your work together, or whether they think that something entirely different is going on. That may be a question you find too risky to ask!

"The decision to take me into care and to put me into the home they put me into was a major one in my life and very traumatic, and I had no part in that and when...my sisters and me were split up...I think that if we had been involved in that decision making process the split wouldn't have been that way." (2)

All the same, it is worth spending some time reminding ourselves about some of the essential components of the consultation process and how to incorporate them into everyday practice. This exercise may help your team to come up with a collective view about it.

TEAM EXERCISE

*   Choose a case in which one or more of the children are about to be provided with accommodation. This doesn't have to be one of your own -ask the duty team, or the training section if you need new ideas.

*   Agree between you on the scenario of admission to accommodation. This can be just the outline of a situation; you are not testing each other on how precise your information is!

*   Divide yourselves into three groups: the family and friends (adults); the child/ren; the social worker. This is not a role play!

Each group to spend 30 minutes working on the following:

i)   ideally, who would the social worker consult with?

ii)   from this list, is everyone essential? If not, say why you think their contribution is less important

iii)   how would the worker go about consulting with each person? (individual meeting, telephone call, etc.)

iv)   brainstorm all the issues which your group believes are the most important to be included in the consultation at this stage; put the first 6 in order of priority

v)   note 3 ways in which your group thinks that the worker can demonstrate that the consultation process is being taken seriously

vi)   what do you think should happen next about any areas of disagreement?

List your feedback on the wall so that you can compare it and then discuss in the whole group:

i)   what are the similarities and differences between the groups' responses and what is significant about them?

ii)   compare your feedback with current practice. What are the implications for different team members, including the team leader and the allocation of resources?

iii)   what were the ethnic, class, disability and other attributes you ascribed to the case study family? What differences to the consultation process did this kind of information make?

Except in emergencies, which should be exceptional, consultation should be routine, should involve all those concerned, should be appropriate to their age and circumstances and should be carefully recorded so that people are assured that they have been properly heard. Good consultation is part of the assessment process discussed in Chapter 3, and proper attention therefore must be paid to the child in the context of family and community, in society, and in relation to the powerful institution which is the social services department. Failure to consult fully may be an indication that the assessment process is being undermined. Such an omission is both short sighted and against all the intention of the legislation to encourage as full a partnership between client and agency as possible. Later decision making will be that much more difficult if views and wishes are not expressed and taken seriously at this stage. More importantly, mistakes and misunderstandings will jeopardise the future well being of the children concerned.

Involving clients goes well beyond simply asking their opinion about, for example, an individual foster carer. It implies that:

*   each person involved is aware of the reason for the provision of accommodation;

*   each person knows that all possible options within the family and friends have been explored before it was decided to look elsewhere for the child to live;

*   each person knows the purpose of the placement, how long it is intended to last and what is planned for the future; and

*   everyone is then *"given adequate information and helped to consider alternatives and contribute to the making of an informed choice about the most appropriate form of care"* (Principles and Practice Guide no.10)

Practitioners' responsibility

The process of consultation is inevitably affected by the power imbalances which are present between, for example, agency and family; white and black people; women and men; adult and child. Generally speaking, however uncertain, unsupported or exhausted they are, workers have considerably greater power than their clients and with it, the responsibility to share that power as far as possible with them. For example, the younger children are, the less power they have to participate in decision-making about their lives, and the less they are used to adult methods of consultation. Some adults, in seeking to relieve youngsters of this responsibility, have underestimated the strength of feeling or understanding that some children have about their situation and of the problems to be resolved. Children find it particularly hard to be assertive with adults when there is a family problem that they think may be their fault, however long standing the problem may be. They need special attention to help them understand the power that they do have, and to use it constructively. (How did the "children" in your team exercise think this could be done? This may involve finding another worker with whom the child feels more at ease, possibly from another workplace or agency, finding the child an advocate from their own family or network to strengthen their position in relation to the agency.)

Many adults are also lacking in power in relation to social work agencies and as such find it hard to express their wishes or disagree with a worker's proposal. There are many parents who feel negatively judged by social workers because they need help, and this sense of being criticised undermines their authority with their children and with the agency, particularly if their children are being cared for by someone else. Those with children with a disability, for example, may feel that the worker believes they were in some way responsible for their child's condition; this fear can quickly dis-empower a competent adult.

In all these situations, it is vital that workers are able to acknowledge that they have a certain amount of power or authority, by virtue of the job, which they have the ability to exert. Sometimes workers themselves are feeling dis-empowered, for personal or professional reasons, and it can be difficult to recognise that this authority still exists, and that it has considerable influence on all relationships with clients.

Policy support

Good practice around placement planning is based, ideally, on sound policy and structural supports. In many agencies, it is the practice which informs and demands policy change and development, which keeps it alive and helps to promote consistent standards throughout the workforce. Such a policy may:

i)   require placement with family and friends to be the first option for any child;

ii)   require proper planning arrangements for each child, including written agreements made with child and family;

iii)   require practitioners to explain fully the nature and availability of any placement choice and to involve the family in assessing its suitability for their child;

iv)   enable practitioners to undertake this consultation on an anti-discriminatory basis; in other words, one which assumes that all clients will be consulted and involved unless there are exceptional circumstances;

v)   involve members of the community in developing and publicising the policy;

vi)   give a training commitment to ensure that staff understand both why and how to undertake such consultation in an anti-discriminatory way;

vii)   produce a representations and complaints procedure which is user-friendly, available in a range of languages, and outlines a problem solving form of mediation as well as the formal procedure ; and

viii)   make available the resources to carry out these responsibilities without cutting corners.

2. CONSULTATION -SKILLS

Ascertaining wishes and feelings

Some practitioners will be comfortable with many aspects of this work. Others may find they reach a stumbling block with some situations and need extra help and guidance. It may be helpful to refer back to the principles and essentials of assessment work referred to in the previous chapter to think about the basis on which the consultation is carried out. Other questions which focus more specifically on discussion around placement include:

i) How many people in the family would you routinely involve in such a discussion?

ii) Whose wishes and feelings would you consider essential and whose optional?

iii) Do you make the same decision about whom to include in every situation; if not, what makes a difference?

iv) Which people, beyond the family, do you routinely consider to be relevant?

v) Do you automatically include other professionals (and if so, does the family know?)

vi) Do you ask the family who else they think should be invited to comment or take part in decision making, such as godparents, friends or advocates?

vii) At what age do you ask a child their wishes and feelings? (No specific age limit as such is given in the Act and practitioners must therefore find out as best they can from all children). How would you define the difference between "asking" a child something and "ascertaining their feelings"? Do you talk to children about placements before, after or at the same time as their parents?

viii) Are you able to communicate with children or adults who, for example, have a hearing or speech impediment?

ix) How do you go about finding out the views of people who speak a different language to you? In these families, do you routinely involve the same people or do you make exceptions or changes because of the language?

Giving due consideration to wishes and feelings

This work can be divided into two stages:

i) understanding what the person has said and being able to understand its significance and relevance

All children complain at some point or another that adults do not listen and do not understand them. This natural communication gap is further widened in the case of children who are troubled or hurt, who need special care and attention to grow. The time needed to do this is a precious resource and it may be that some people are better placed than the social worker to find out how a child feels and what she or he wants to happen. The ability to allow others to share this responsibility is as important as the ability to acknowledge the need to discuss with others the significance of the information gathered.

For example, a couple whose first baby is born with a severe handicap may refuse to have anything to do with him and insist that someone else looks after him; a skilled worker, experienced in dealing with the shock, grief and anger of such parents will need to assess the significance of their expressed wishes at each stage.

Similarly, a child whose mother has died, and whose father, not previously living with them, is not able to look after her, may also be overwhelmed with grief and anger and may change her mind considerably about her living arrangements over a period of several months.

In all situations, as with all stages in the

assessment process, the worker must place the child and family in the context of their ethnic background, class and culture, and in the context of the social worker's perceptions and attitudes and the power of the agency. Some of these factors will change, or be changed over time, and the consultation process will reflect this dynamic.

ii)   recording that information and accurately and appropriately incorporating it into the work.

The duty to give due consideration to wishes and feelings, coupled with the new representations procedures, may afford families the opportunity to complain if they believe that they have been insufficiently heard and paid attention to. (See Chapter 2 for discussion about setting up the procedures) Good shared recording and access to files policies will therefore be essential, as will training and guidelines, to assist staff.

For example, managers must decide whether it will be sufficient for the social workers to record a child's wishes in the case file, or to have discussed them with the supervisor. Other methods of recording may be thought more appropriate, such as tape recordings or a combination of drawings and words.

Alongside other standard forms regarding the arrangement of the placement, there should be a form on which all those concerned record their views about the accommodation to be provided, about the plans being made and about work which needs to be done. It will also record areas of disagreement and can be used by the practitioner to show either how these were resolved, or compromises made, or decisions made where no compromise could be reached.

The use of such agreements and shared records are strongly encouraged by the Department of Health, social work researchers, advocates, practitioners and those representing the views of clients and foster carers (3)(4)

The Children Act's requirements to share parental responsibility, share decision making, work co-operatively between agencies, make plans clear to the court, enable people to use procedures to voice disagreements and other duties all clearly indicate that the legislators are looking for greatly improved practice in this area. It has been a matter of concern for some time that many families may have a child in care, voluntarily or against their wishes, living away from home with perhaps minimal contact, and yet have not one piece of written information about their legal position or that of their child, nor about the child's current health and well being, and plans for the future. Given the serious and significant nature of all such situations, it is astonishing that any agency should need to be reminded or encouraged to give children and their families such written information.

Written agreements

The use of written agreements with families is a further step towards good practice and should only be used in a positive and practical way. They do not in themselves carry any kind of guarantee, either for worker or family, of a better relationship between them, an improvement in child care or more sensitive social work practice. They will be as relevant, helpful and constructive as the worker who initiates them, and as such are an indicator rather than a guarantee of good practice. The construction and content of the agreement will in particular demonstrate the extent to which the worker has acknowledged the power of her or his agency and of her or his own position in relation to the client. In understanding the imbalance which is an integral part of that relationship, she or he then decides on the extent and nature of their power sharing.

The use of agreements is viewed favourably as a way of avoiding "drift"; that is of children continuing to be looked after by a local authority, or coming in and out of accommodation, without clear plans being made for them. However, workers need to be aware that the whole concept of such agreements assumes that the client and

Chapter 4

Social Work Agencies and children who are looked after

worker:

* share a common understanding of the problem(s)

* have a degree of mutual trust

* have a common way of expressing themselves (usually direct verbal expression of problem recognition and possible resolution)

* have a shared understanding of time, and

* have a broadly similar view of the context in which the problem has arisen.

For example: a 15 year old Asian girl has been found by the police in a town 20 miles from her home. She has been shoplifting for some time and had tried to run away from home several times after arguments with her parents about her white English boyfriend. They had previously asked for advice about the stealing. The white male social worker who visits the family decides that the problem is one of a clash of cultures between the girl and her strict, conventional parents, and feels that they will have to do some work to understand the world in which their daughter is growing up. It is agreed that the girl will stay in the residential home on a short term basis, and that a written agreement will be used to negotiate a build up of trust between the family again, so that the girl can gradually be allowed more freedom.

In this case, it is obvious that this agreement will fail, because attention to the points made above are missing. The social worker has made an instant and uncorroborated assumption about cultural clashes being at the root of this problem. In this case, he also failed to focus the agreement on the problem about which the parents were most concerned, which was the shoplifting. He has not addressed crucial issues about an Asian family dealing with a white organisation and thought about how their attitudes and feelings towards the system in which their daughter is enmeshed may be affecting them, nor how his personal racism has distorted the situation and therefore made the work untenable. Finally, he has not ac-

knowledged to the girl the power issues involved in their relationship deriving from their race, gender, and age differences nor attempted to include other workers or relevant adults to help with this.

This example, albeit a superficial one, shows that written agreements cannot be used to coerce families into making any kind of plans which are not based on their version of what is really happening. Whilst worker and family are in the process of getting to know each other, however, they can be very useful for making short term, concrete plans, even in emergencies, and as such can serve to reassure child, parents and carers that matters are under control and that the child is safe. Clear agency guidelines about their use and status are needed to avoid undermining behaviour by the worker and to assure clients of the value of such agreements.

Written Agreement Guidelines may include:

1. A positive statement against agency racism which forms the basis for a respectful partnership with black and minority ethnic clients.

2. The automatic inclusion of free translating and interpreting services will assure clients that their need of such services is not a problem.

3. The free provision of a signer, lipreader or Braille writer should be automatically offered.

4. Clients must be informed that any agreement does not have the status of a legal contract, and therefore is not legally binding. However, they should be warned that in any situation in which there is concern for a child's welfare, and from which legal action may ensue, the agreement may be brought in evidence in court proceedings by any party. (e.g. to show that the parent acted unreasonably.)

5. The agreement should be based on the assumption that the work is being shared and that there will be tasks for everyone, including the agency worker.

6. The agreement should be time limited, with a review date agreed by all at a mutually convenient time.

7. The agreement should be able to be varied at the request of anyone involved, even the youngest child, by further discussion. It is no good sticking to something which clearly isn't going to work and which reinforces feelings of failure and inadequacy.

8. Sanctions for breaking the agreement need to be clear. Many social workers make so-called agreements which are actually just a list of ways in which the client's behaviour must improve in order to avoid court proceedings to have the child removed. Sometimes, neither the required behaviour change, nor the sanction, is clearly spelt out, as in this example:

"Parental contract re: Sean

1. *We understand that whilst Sean is in care we are expected to co-operate fully with the Social Services Department via the social worker, Ms Garland.*

2. *We will visit Sean or have him home on a regular basis.*

3. *We will attend necessary meetings in the interests of Sean, Ray and ourselves.*

4. *We understand that it is necessary to show a commitment towards Sean to enable rehabilitation to work. We also understand that lack of commitment may mean that Social Services would have to take steps towards a secure future for Sean."*

This example of an actual contract (names changed) is taken from "Using written agreements with children and families", Family Rights Group.

Sanctions should be applicable also to the social worker and other professionals, who otherwise appear to be completely unaccountable if they do not complete their tasks. It will be very important for some families that it is clearly recorded if, for example, plans for contact failed not because they were uninterested but because the worker did not provide the fares in advance as agreed.

9. It should be possible to appeal against the contents of an agreement. It has sometimes been very difficult for family members to voice their unhappiness or anger for the simple reasons that either there is no-one independent to complain to or there is too much at stake and they are afraid of the consequences. Practitioners must understand that it isn't enough to tell someone that they can complain to their (the worker's) line manager, or a young person to their key worker. No service user can have confidence in the impartiality of such a system. Under the Children Act, the new representations procedures must include an independent person and this may provide clients with the route they need to be sure of fair agreements.

Social Work Agencies and children who are looked after

ORGANISATION EXERCISE

* What policy, if any, does your agency have about the use of written agreements with clients?

* Is there any team, establishment or individual who is currently using agreements and could discuss their practice with your team?

* Ask the training section to arrange a course.

* Contact national organisations for material or advice. (for example NFCA, FRG, NAYPIC)

* Contact local parents' groups and other service users to ask for their views about the use of agreements; there may be problems you hadn't thought of, or situations in which they would welcome their use.

TEAM EXERCISE

*   Return to the case study you used for the exercise on consultation (p95)

*   Divide into the same groups. Work out an agreement to cover:

a) the first 7 days of the placement
b) the first 4 weeks of the placement

The agreement should include :

a statement of the problem,
what needs to happen to resolve the problem,
who needs to do what, and by when
sanctions,
arrangements for disagreements and review.

It may be helpful to do this in the separate groups initially and then compare notes.

*   In doing this exercise, what has arisen as a result of the similarities and differences between worker and family/friends, in terms of ethnic background, culture, class, gender and so on which has helped or hindered this process? How can you build on the strengths you have in the team, and what can you do about the problems you have identified?

PERSONAL EXERCISE

*   Make a list of your current caseload.

*   In cases where you are not using written agreements, put in order of priority the ones where you think you could.

*   What steps can you take to begin this work with these families or individuals? Who can help you, what supports or guidance will you need?

*   If you are able to, discuss with your team leader or a colleague why, in some situations, you do not feel able to use agreements. If the obstacles are insurmountable for you, would it be possible, and helpful, for someone else to undertake this part of your work, either with or without you?

RACIAL ORIGIN

In Chapter 3, the centrality of a child's race, culture, religion and language was explored in relation to assessment work. In providing accommodation for children and looking after them, these factors come into very sharp focus in relation to the direct provision which an agency makes for those children who are unable to live with their usual carers.

a) Giving "due consideration" to racial origin means:

i) understanding the connection between race and decision-making in this context and

ii) applying that understanding to an individual child and the decision which is to be made with or for her or him.

The second point relies on the first. Practitioners who are initiating or developing anti-discriminatory work will be aware that you cannot start with an individual case and work backwards to the principle, because you may find that the principle has shifted or disappeared altogether. The result is inevitably disorganised, inconsistent practice which is vulnerable under pressure.

The reason why racial origin must be addressed is straightforward: our society is racist in many different ways, and within that wider context, our child care systems are based on assumptions of the superiority of white race and culture. Therefore, any child who, for reasons of racial origin, is not considered to be a full member of the superior group, must be exposed to the message that she or he is inferior by virtue of parentage, skin colour or cultural heritage. Children in this position who need to be looked after by strangers are vulnerable to the decision-making process of a system which is not primarily about or for them and which will therefore tend to reinforce rather than redress this perceived inferiority. The administrators of this system - social

workers, residential and foster carers, teachers, police - are predominantly from society's favoured racial group and none of them, however sympathetic or aware, will ever fully understand the experience of a black child. White workers, because of the society and system within which they work and for which to a certain extent they are each responsible and of which each are representatives, have an exceptional responsibility towards black children who need their help. This sense of responsibility cannot be based on guilt, pity or curiosity, although many white social workers will have experienced these emotions at some time or another, but rather should derive from a hard headed conviction that racism exists in child care work as it does elsewhere, that it is always destructive, and that it must always be fought in every way possible.

Black workers involved in the same process of decision-making about children who are looked after are in a very different position due to the experience of racism, which they share with black children, the added experience of being black adults in a white organisation and the different power relationship which this put them into with their black and white clients. It has been acknowledged that they are undermined and marginalised. (See Chapter 1). Whatever their own professional and personal experience black workers are necessarily caught up in a tremendously complex web of their own and other people's expectations about what they can and ought to do in working with black children and their families.

In making decisions about children who are looked after therefore, paying due consideration to their racial origin involves more than simply working out whether same race foster carers are available or whether the residential home staff know anything about the political situation in Ethiopia, or can cook rice and peas. It means that all staff and carers must know why this question is important and be prepared to take action, whatever their job, to tackle the inequalities which arise. As always, this is easier to do if there is an agency policy which positively

Chapter 4

Social Work Agencies and children who are looked after

encourages all staff to be anti-racist and is prepared to tackle those who aren't, through discussions, training and disciplinary action when necessary. Perhaps only a minority of social service agencies have such a firm commitment; where this doesn't exist, alternative networks of support within and across agency boundaries are even more important.

CHECKPOINT

*   Do you, your colleagues and your agency share a common understanding of the language and concepts of race and racism?

Even if your agency has a policy which you believe is founded on anti-racist principles, there is no doubt that it will be being used extremely variably by your colleagues and being abused or ignored by others. Some social work agencies continue to deny the need for such a policy.

*   What can you do about any of this and what supports will you need? You may be able to make small changes within your team or office; challenge racism in one specific area of your work; campaign to get some forms or procedures amended; suggest alternative assessment methods or the inclusion of people from outside the agency to help.

*   If you believe that there are problems with the agency's policies, think about contacting outside organisations which may be able to support proposals for change; for example: REU, CRE, Black and In Care, SSI, BAAF, NFCA.

---

b) Same race placements

An agency's commitment to making same race placements will depend on its ideological stance, not just on its resources. The extent of that commitment will partly depend on the distinction it makes between believing that all children are generally better off being raised by people who are like them, and understanding that black children need to be raised by black adults in order to grow in a psychologically healthy way in this society.

Much confusion and misunderstanding has arisen over the use of the word "race". It has passed into common usage to denote simply the difference between black and white peoples, and can only have a limited advantage when workers are trying to elicit more accurate information. In many situations, practitioners will find it more accurate and appropriate to use "ethnic origin". In this discussion, children of mixed parentage where one parent is black, are considered to be black. What is important in this context is that when we are discussing same race placements, or finding a family of the same ethnic origin, we are almost always talking about the placement needs of black children. This is because white children have far less difficulty in being placed with families of the same ethnic origin, and even if they did, they would not experience racism in that process. Black children, however, have for years been placed in white families and many have experienced severe problems as a result; their difficulties are specific and are in relation to their identity, self esteem, confidence and ability to function in society on reaching maturity.

"I feel bitter towards my social worker who never thought about my position as a black person in a white society, who never thought that at 16 I'd start asking questions. ...People were going further than keeping me away from my community, they were turning me against my whole community...my own skin." (5)

Some children learn to deny their colour to the extent that they believe that they are white, or go to extreme lengths to try and turn themselves white by bleaching and scrubbing their skin. (6)

"I didn't know what to do because I was the only one there...I tried to be more like them although I knew I was black, I wanted to be black, but they

made it so difficult for me because they didn't seem to understand it....in a way I was invisible." (7)

This identity denial or confusion is compounded by the fact that, living only with white adults, they are unable to learn, from the first hand, day to day experience of others, how to develop and maintain their self esteem, identity and self respect in a racist society.

"The head of home was a black woman and things started to look up.. we started to have positive images given to us actually in the place we was sleeping...we started living there mentally... she empowered us to go out there and fight the day." (8)

The only way to avoid these particular problems arising, with their consequent psychological trauma, is to avoid placing black children with white carers. The D.o.H. gives cautious agreement:- *" families of similar ethnic origin are also normally best placed to prepare children for life as members of an ethnic minority group in a multi -racial society, where they may meet with racial prejudice and discrimination, and to help them with their development toward independent living and adult life." (9)*

The beginning of the 1980s saw the first serious attempt to recruit black families for black children through initiatives such as the New Black Families Unit co-run by the Independent Adoption Society and London Borough of Lambeth. The projects proved that it was possible to find suitable black families and they continued to assess and approve and place children with them. (10)

Even the most committed agency may find that it is not always possible to place a child with a foster family of the same ethnic background, especially in the case of mixed parentage children, or in areas where the minority ethnic population is tiny, although it must be said that finding an exact match is not the only strategy in an anti-racist policy. Decisions have to be taken balanc-

ing children's need for an ethnically "suitable" family with their need to move from what may be unsuitable short term accommodation and to feel settled, and will be part of an assessment about the foster family's ability to provide the child with a positive identity as a black person. What will quickly become essential will be good links with the local black communities so that they are informed about the need for fostering, and confident of their abilities to provide for those children.

The recruitment of black families is discussed by the British Agencies for Adoption and Fostering(11); they suggest incorporating the following into publicity strategies:

1. aim directly at your target group

2. know your target area

3. use the media

4. overcome the language barrier

5. make direct connnections

6. ensure that initial contacts are positive

This kind of campaign then needs to be supported by careful assessment work, preparation and post placement groups and constant monitoring and readiness to take on change.

Recruitment of transracial carers or adopters is an especially demanding task, especially for workers who do not believe that this is the best way forward for black children. In 1986, John Small outlined the ingredients which he considered necessary in any substitute home for black children, given the dynamics of transracial placements.(12) He laid out guidelines for the selection and preparation of appropriate carers and questions to be asked about their attitudes and environment. These could usefully form the basis for a discussion in any home finding team which is faced with these dilemmas.

Social Work Agencies and children who are looked after

ORGANISATION EXERCISE

*   What is your agency's policy and practice regarding same-race placements?

*   Do you each have a copy of the D.o.H.'s guidance (13)?

*   Will your policy be in line with the new duties contained in the Children Act to give due consideration to racial origin?

*   What can you do to influence your agency's policy? This may include getting advice from national organisations such as NFCA and BAAF; contacting other agencies to discuss positive ways to promote anti-racist policies; talking to black carers and parents to hear their views and hold meetings with managers and elected members.

TEAM EXERCISE

*   Return to the exercise you did on consultation on p. 95 . If you haven't done this one, then choose a family or make one up in which accommodation is to be provided for one or more of the children.

*   Divide yourselves into three groups: the adult family members/friends, the children and social worker. Again, this is not a role play.

*   **Each group to spend 30 minutes working on the following:**

i)   what is the racial origin (or ethnicity) of the child/ren to be accommodated?

ii)   social workers: in what ways (be as specific as you can) would you show that you had paid due consideration to that racial origin? What are your preferred options and what are your alternatives? How would the family know that you had done any of this?

iii)   adult family members and children: in what ways would you expect the social worker to give due consideration to the child/ren's racial origin? What would be your preferred options and your alternatives? How would you know that the social worker had paid due consideration and what could you do if you disagree?

-    **List your feedback on the wall so that you can compare it and then discuss in the whole group:**

i)   what are the similarities and differences between the groups' responses and what is significant about them?

ii)   compare your feedback with current practice. What are the implications for different team members, including the team leader and the allocation of resources?

iii)   decide on the steps you will take within the team to develop your practice; include in this a timetable for changes and supports you will need.

CULTURAL BACKGROUND

In order to give due consideration to a child's cultural background, a social worker needs to:

*   recognise that everyone has a culture;

*   know that cultures are different, not superior or inferior;

*   recognise that "culture" is not a static concept and is constantly evolving for individuals, families and communities;

*   understand the significance of different cultures in the context of the decision to be made;

*   avoid stereotyping; and

*   make the appropriate connections with the child's race, religion and language.

All of us have an identifiable culture, just as we all have a racial origin. Cultural identity is a powerful force in anyone's life, affecting our attitudes and behaviour towards child rearing, work, marriage, education, and money amongst others. It is also very powerful in our wider relationships between social and family groups, communities, regions and countries. In Britain, the dominance of one particular social group is not just based on their skin colour but also on the culture, religion and language attributed to that group. There are many clues which we all give each other to help us place strangers in their 'correct' group; having placed them we apply our learned response and experience to shape our behaviour towards them.

There is much written and talked about our "multi-cultural" society and about the need to respect and learn about each others' ways. Whilst this is important, what matters first for social workers is being prepared to recognise the discrimination that takes place in cultural evaluation, including, in this context, towards children who need to be looked after outside of their network of family and friends. This is important in order to carry out the principle of avoiding further discrimination against those children who already experience it in their everyday lives.

(Principles and Practice Guide no.21)

Stereotyping by cultural characteristics

Many black and minority ethnic people have to fight continuous battles to avoid sweeping generalisations about their cultural characteristics, such as :

> "Caribbean families are matriarchal"
> "Gypsies don't believe in education"
> "Asians are good at business but work very long hours"

These are cultural stereotypes based on race and country of origin, and have no more meaning or logic than saying:

> "Europeans like football" or
> "English families are small and isolated from distant relatives"

Other stereotypes are based on:
class
"working class men like beer and football"

money
"poor people just don't budget properly"

gender
"girls prefer to play with dolls, not cars"

sexual identity
"gay men can't be good fathers"

disability
"how can deaf children enjoy music?"

employment status
"the long-term unemployed are feckless"

Cultural stereotypes are often derogatory, defining what a group of people do, are imagined to do or cannot do as a result of belonging to that group. What matters for children in this context is that their social workers are able to accurately recognise their cultural clues, link them with other vital information, and understand how the accommodation to be provided must be part of work which:

i)   avoids furthering any discrimination children have suffered, and

ii)   promotes a healthy pride and awareness in children of their cultural identity, and hence their healthy and assertive development .

Social Work
Agencies and
children who are
looked after

FOR EXAMPLE:

BACKGROUND:

a white working class single parent has to go into hospital because of problems with her third pregnancy. Her mother would normally care for the children but is ill. Due to complications, her hospital stay is extended until the birth, a total of about 4 months. Her son has severe asthma and bronchitis and attends a special school. Her part-time job is not secure and she needs advice on social security benefits. The children's father, who has remarried and has two more children, has regular but infrequent contact with them and pays low maintenance. Her daughter aged 7 and son aged 5 are placed together in a white middle class family.

Cultural clues: white family; poor; working class; single parent; probably heterosexual; child with disability; English language; father not directly involved ; grandmother important but ill.

Negative evaluation:

- mother seen as irresponsible for having third child with no male partner around

- mother seen as difficult because of problems in pregnancy

- father seen as irresponsible because of infrequent visits and low maintenance

- children suffering due to low income, having few clothes and books, need more heating at home

- son seen as either a problem or a victim because of his poor health; either way, may need rescuing from the situation

Practical outcome of negative evaluation:

- social worker and carer see this as opportunity to smarten up the children by providing new clothes, getting haircuts, buying 'suitable' books and educational toys

- money is made available to fund the above

- the children are asked questions about their father's visits, whether they love him, about his new family, and about their mother and her male friends

- the children are discouraged from watching their usual TV programmes, mealtime habits are different and they have less responsibility than at home

- visits to their mother and sick grandmother are given less priority than those to the foster family's relatives

- visits to the mother are reduced after the son's asthma gets worse after seeing her

- foster carer has discussions with teacher and doctor about son's asthma and bronchitis and possible new kinds of treatment

- no advice given regarding benefits, as any extra would be wasted by poor management

Positive evaluation:

- mother treated with respect for being able to raise children by herself

- understanding that parents have worked out the visiting arrangement which is best for their two families

- mother respected for managing in chronic poverty, to feed and clothe the children, and to keep debts in manageable proportions

- problems in the pregnancy seen in context of poverty and mother's general poor health and exhaustion

- understanding that children have level of responsibility which is appropriate for their family

Practical outcome of positive evaluation:

- mother encouraged to make as many decisions as possible about the children, such as which clothes to buy if there is money for this; to continue to deal with school as usual

- detailed negotiations held between mother, worker and carer about normal rules of behaviour, discipline and so on, with mother's wishes taken fully into account

- meetings held at the hospital

- all arrangements confirmed in writing to everyone concerned

- children's own culture respected, by encouraging them to bring and use own toys, books, watch usual TV

- father and mother consulted together about any changes to his visiting plans

- visits to mother and grandmother a priority, with additional work to comfort and reassure son

- no consultation with other professionals without mother's full knowledge and consent

- advice given regarding social security benefits as social worker recognises that every extra gained is well directed.

The effect of living in a 'multi-cultural' society is different for all children in Britain. For many, there is little overt influence on their lifestyle and upbringing because they are amongst the broadly dominant group which is white, able-bodied, English, Christian and living in hetero-sexual nuclear family units. They, in effect, live in a mono-cultural society with multi-cultural overtones. Other children grow up in a dual or multi-cultural family or neighbourhood and will have learned from adults and other children how to adapt to these different influences. The common experience this latter group have is that their primary culture is somehow at variance with the main culture of their contemporaries. The challenge for each is to learn how to value equally the different influences and experiences which surround them. This is the same challenge which confronts practitioners who are offering them a service.

Chapter 4

*Social Work
Agencies and
children who are
looked after*

ORGANISATION EXERCISE

*   What are the dominant cultural characteristics of your organisation? (e.g. able-bodied, female, religious/secular)

*   On what information have you based your answer? (e.g. breakdown of staff in your office, policies, anecdote)

*   Do the dominant cultures of your agency reflect those of your clients? In which ways are they alike and different, and how does this affect the service your agency offers?

TEAM EXERCISE

This is a list of some cultural clues with which we identify some people in Britain. Work out which clues would:

*   place a child or family in an identifiable group

*   look at the groups you have come up with; do any of your team members think that they belong in these groups? What are the negative stereotypes which you think are attributed to them, and how would you want to challenge these?

leaving school at 16	monthly salary	children to bed at early hour
large print stories	dhal and rice	nanny
working mother	boarding school	TV soaps
black skin girls	bible	free school meals
red hair	burger and chips	unemployment benefit
single homeless	own computer	divorced parents
braids	public school	vegan
laundrette	rap	wheelchair
synagogue		

PERSONAL EXERCISE

Work out your own cultural origin.
Are you part of a dominant culture in Britain?
In which ways?

In which ways do you conform to the dominant cultures of your organisation and in which ways do you differ? How does this affect your position or practice at work? (e.g. with your colleagues, chances of promotion, loyalty to the organisation)

What does this knowledge mean for your professional practice and your relationships with your clients?

RELIGIOUS PERSUASION

a) Social work background

The social work profession in Britain derives itself from an overtly Christian background. The Victorian philanthropists and middle class "lady almoners" were, on the whole, staunchly religious and their doctrines and beliefs have profoundly influenced the development of social work education and practice. Christianity, money and class were a powerful combination, and so that influence was widespread and long-lasting in the form of endowments, trusts and organisational aims, some of which continue today, especially in the voluntary sector. A number of charities, some large and influential, identify themselves as having a Christian foundation. In the local authorities, however, social work tends, on the whole, to be a more secular profession.

During the 1970s and early 1980s, there were shifts in some social work training courses towards Marxist and feminist ideologies, which had considerable influence on the attitudes and politics of the workforce thereafter. It was the decade of growth in self-help and advocacy groups, of the women's liberation movement, of changing social and moral values and a greater awareness of the diversity of faiths and cultures which are currently influential in Britain, although it also bred a certain amount of religious intolerance in some workers.

At the beginning of the 1990s, Britain is still called a Christian country, and most of its citizens would probably identify themselves as such, although only a minority are active in the faith. Social workers, along with teachers and other professionals, have needed to become more knowledgeable about other religious beliefs in areas where some members of the local population are not Christian. These are also most likely to be areas of high black and minority ethnic populations. Many practitioners still know very little about the actual tenets of faiths

other than Christianity, but may have learned a considerable amount about the moral code and culture surrounding the religion, including rules of behaviour between family members, the place of holy days in a child's life, the significance of dress, diet and so on.

b) Religious discrimination

When children are to be provided with accommodation by a local authority, voluntary organisation or registered children's home, the social worker must find out and pay due consideration to their religious persuasion. As with racial origin, culture and language, this information can be meaningless without putting it into the context of the child's family, community and wider society; and without the practitioner also being aware of what that information conveys to her or him. Every child identified as Christian, for example, is a member of society's dominant religious faith. However, being a member of the dominant faith does not prevent discrimination against some people, and this is more likely to affect the parents and other adult relatives than the child, at least in the first instance. For example, belonging to some Christian sects, such as the Plymouth Brethren, can exclude them from that position; being Catholic is likely to mean very different things to those brought up in England, Ireland or Chile.

Social work can be intolerant of those who are "extreme" or "too fixed" in their Christianity and is ready to attribute negative moral influences on children as a result. Some black families have suffered acute intolerance from white workers unsympathetic to their Pentecostalist worship; "Ironic", as one black woman said, "that you white people told us to believe in the Bible and now you don't like the way we're doing it." Not only ironic but ambivalent or even hypocritical, when workers from the same agencies may be actively trying to recruit black foster carers through the church.

Another black woman with two grandchil-

Chapter

Social Work Agencies and children who are looked after

dren then in care, complained to her advocate that the white foster carer, also Christian, had told the white social worker that the children's prayers were "inappropriate", and they had agreed, without consulting the grandmother, that they should be changed. Racism and religious prejudice constantly overlap and situations such as this can undermine children's racial pride as well as their religious understanding and enjoyment; in this case, it badly affected the strength and authority of the grandmother, who found it difficult to assert herself in rehabilitation arrangements.

c) Organisational policies

Social work practitioners need clear guidelines about their agency policy in the placement of children which takes account of their religion. For example, if the agency aims to place children with foster carers of the same religion, how much priority should they normally give this? The Children Act does not lay the same duties on local authorities to have regard to the religions of children in need, as it does to racial origin when recruiting foster carers and arranging day care (sch 2. (11)) Does this exclusion mean that it has less meaning in the interpretation of "due consideration?" On the other hand, social workers were already legally bound, before the Act was passed, to place children with a foster carer of the same religion, or, if that were not practicable, with a foster carer who undertook that the child would be brought up in that religion. (14)

The Department of Health, in its letter of January 1990 to directors of social service departments, says that *"sustained efforts may be needed to recruit a sufficient number and range of foster parents and prospective adopters... of particular religious affiliations, such efforts being essential if all children who need substitute families are to have the opportunity of placement within families which share their ethnic origin and religion."*

Further on the document states: *"The importance of religion as an element of culture should never be overlooked: to some children and fami-*

lies it may be the dominant factor, so that the religion of foster parents or adopters may in some cases be more important than their ethnic origin." (15)

Practitioners and managers in home finding teams, those involved in placing children and those who sit on fostering and adoption panels may want to re-phrase this statement in a way which makes more sense for themselves and children, avoiding the possibility of unhelpful comparisons with the importance of same race placements.

In many families, religion is important in its own right, not as an "element of culture". Here, religious belief forms the foundation stone of family life and the culture which develops and grows outward from it; in this sense, religion and culture are an integral part of each other. These factors combine to make up an essential part of a child's identity and life experience and as such cannot be separated from her or his ethnicity.

d) Giving due consideration to religious persuasion - some practical implications

All practitioners:

ORGANISATION EXERCISE

* Find out the religious persuasion and family practice of every child who has been placed within the agency, at your establishment or by your team within the past year.

  If this information is not recorded, find out who in the organisation will be responsible for monitoring after the implementation of the Children Act.

  If the information is recorded, find out if the children were placed with carers of the same religion.

* Does your agency have a policy about religion and placement? Does it reflect current views and practice?

* How will your agency ensure that, after implementation, religious persuasion and practice will be routinely given proper consideration at assessment, placement and in conferences and reviews?

EXERCISE WITH COLLEAGUES

* Each person write down up to 5 words describing the attitude of the team to having a religious faith, as they perceive or experience it. Put the words in a box. Each person to draw out a word in turn, read and put on a board. When all the words are out, each person to think of something which the team can do to sustain positive attitudes, change negative attitudes or remedy ignorance.

  For example, "liberal tolerance" may imply a certain laziness and lack of understanding about the extent of religious hostility experienced by some people. A worker might suggest that the team builds on its basically positive attitude by finding examples of religious intolerance, thinking about how this may affect team members, clients and colleagues and about how this will inform their work.

* Discuss how the culture within your team encourages or suppresses acknowledgement of religious belief by workers. Are they enabled to understand and discuss the connections between their religion and their work? Are those with a minority belief expected to act as specialist advisers to clients and colleagues?

Chapter 4

Social Work Agencies and children who are looked after

PERSONAL EXERCISE

* As a child, were you raised in a religious faith? What are your memories of that? Do you have a belief now?
If so, is it the same as that in which you were raised?

* Do you share your belief with your family? What are the differences or connections between you about religion? What is the effect on family discussions, decisions, religious holidays, secrets, confidences?

* Do you think that it is a good thing for children to be raised in a religious faith? If so, why, and if not, why not?

* Do you have strong feelings or views about any religion other than your own or the one you were raised in? What are they?

* How do your own experience, political and personal views affect your perceptions and judgements about others' religious beliefs and practice? Are you conscious of this influence on your work and do you find a way to raise it in your supervision or report writing? Think about how you can become more aware of this and find a supportive work colleague to discuss the implications for your practice.

* Do you view spirituality differently to religion? How would you define it and where might it have a place in these discussions?

TEAM EXERCISES

A. FOR PRACTITIONERS WHO RECRUIT FOSTER CARERS AND ADOPTERS

* Does your team have a policy about placing children with carers of the same religious belief or about ensuring that beliefs and practices are respected and upheld?

* Do you have information about the most needed carers in terms of religious belief?

* How does this policy connect with your policies on same race placements and on equal opportunities?

* Devise a positive recruitment policy based on the above information and work out the implications for your team ; (e.g: reorganising priorities, new publicity ideas, training needs.)

B. FOR PRACTITIONERS IN RESIDENTIAL ESTABLISHMENTS

* Do you know the religious faith of all the children in your establishment? Is there a presumption of Christianity, or of no religion if a belief is not expressed?

* Do you know the faith of all staff members?

* What is the culture about religion in your establishment? (e.g: respectful, curious, indifferent, hostile. Has it ever been discussed as a staff issue so that those with a faith find it acceptable to be open about the relationship between their beliefs and their work?)

* Are non-Christians segregated from joint activities, or do children learn positively from each other? e.g: at a boarding school for children with disabilities, there was one Moslem child with a severe hearing loss. The other children learned his prayers so that they could say them together at assembly.

* What are the training and practice implications of this for your colleagues? Include how religious practices are incorporated into the daliy life of your establishment.

C. FOR FIELDWORK PRACTITIONERS

* Do you know the religious faith of all your clients? In what circumstances would you ask them? Is there a presumption of Christianity or of no religion if no preference is expressed?

* When finding out a child's faith, do you ask the child or her parents/carers? Would you routinely find out the beliefs of other family members? In what circumstances would you do this?

* What is the significance, in terms of social work decision making and service provision, of finding out a child's religious persuasion?

* Devise a criteria for satisfying a "due consideration" standard which team members would find acceptable if applied to themselves and their families.

* What are the training and practice implications for you and your colleagues?

Chapter 4

Social Work Agencies and children who are looked after

The centrality of language

The inclusion of linguistic background in a primary piece of child care legislation is an important reminder both of the multiplicity of languages being spoken or understood by British children and the centrality of language in decision making about any child. As with much else which is either required or expected of practice from the Children Act, paying attention to a child's linguistic background will already be well established for many practitioners and their agencies. This can be measured in a number of ways, such as having multi-lingual publicity and written information readily available, multi-lingual reception staff and ensuring the recruitment or training of multi- lingual social workers. Once again, we find that good practice needs to be supported by sound agency policies and the commitment of resources, and because translation and interpreting services are costly, the commitment must be strong and sustainable.

The underlying philosophy which informs that commitment is that any work undertaken by a social services, health or education agency with a child and family is important and may be deeply significant and long lasting; and that no such work should take place without the full and informed understanding and the greatest possible participation of that child and family. Given this premise, it is unthinkable to try and carry out even the shortest assessment of a problem if any of those involved cannot understand each other. There would be no guarantee that any such assessment, or decision which resulted from it, would be either accurate or effective. There is no room, in this work, to make such mistakes. Unfortunately, there are many examples of this having happened, especially where racial or cultural stereotypes have remained unchallenged. The misunderstandings are exacerbated by poor communication.

Policy and practice guidance

If an organisation accepts this philosophy, then there are a number of ways in which it might express it:

i)   a public statement about the positive benefits of a multi-lingual society;

ii)   a statement about the connections between linguistic, racial, cultural and religious prejudice;

iii)   a statement about the organisation's philosophy of providing equal access to services;

iv)   monitoring languages spoken and written within its area;

v)   monitoring languages spoken and written by its staff;

vi)   calculating the cost of services to be initiated or developed and allocating the appropriate budget; lobbying elsewhere for funds.

This initial stage might then be developed by:

Policy guidance for staff, including:

i)   all languages spoken, written or understood by children, their immediate carers and others important to them should be recorded;

ii)   no child or adult should be prevented from understanding and taking part in work with the agency because of a language barrier;

iii)   the onus for overcoming any barrier rests with the agency, not the client;

iv)   the cost of any translation or interpreting services will be borne by the organisation;

v)   any written material provided to children and families should be made available in their first language, or another of their choice; and

vi)   if the social worker does not speak the client's language, then she/he should arrange for an interpreter to be made available at all interviews. (This person may be chosen by the client or employed by the agency. It is vitally important that the client has confidence in the accuracy, understanding and discretion of the interpreter and that clients understand that they have a choice in her or his appointment. Some people will have particular wishes which should be respected, such as an intepreter of the same sex. If necessary, appointments should be adjourned until someone suitable is available, unless of course the child is at immediate risk. Children should not be used to intepret for their parents or other carers.)

A senior manager delegated to undertake the following tasks:

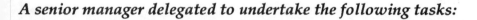

i)   set up monitoring and reviewing procedures regarding the languages of children accommodated and their families;

ii)   set up a forum with clients, self-help groups and others from the community to discuss ways in which the organisation can improve its language services to children and families; e.g.by arranging meetings between parents of children being looked after and who share a common language, to discuss their relationship with the agency and to ensure that they are fully informed of their rights and responsibilities and are aware of departmental and legal procedures;

iii)   administer the budget for translating and interpreting services;

iv)   initiate and develop translation of publicity about the department's services;

v)   devise routine monitoring on assessment, placement and review forms;

vi)   recruit and co-ordinate pool of interpreters, providing training as necessary in child care matters and support to deal with the confidential and sometimes distressing nature of the work;

vii)   meet with interested multi-lingual staff to discuss agency policy and provision, with a clear understanding that this work is not to be imposed on any staff, including section 11-funded workers.

Encouragement to staff and carers to learn new languages.

Area teams to have "fact files" on local and national resources which are multi-lingual, such as law centres, welfare rights offices and community groups. A worker to be designated to update the file and ensure it is easily accessible to the public.

This agency level work will help to support individual and team practice, and vice versa. Some practitioners will be working in organisations which are unsympathetic to the need for automatic and widespread translating and interpreting services and they may need to encourage local parents and organised advocacy groups to pressure councillors about the importance to families - including voters - of this provision.

In addition, workers can check on their own practice and put pressure on their seniors and area mangers to provide a better service in individual cases by arguing that the provision is necessary in order to meet their legal obligation to give due consideration to the child's linguistic background.

PERSONAL OR TEAM EXERCISE

* How many languages are spoken or written by the workers in your team/office/establishment?

* How many languages are spoken or written by the children you work with and their families?

* What do you usually do when you don't have the same language in common?

* Using the following case example, work out a positive strategy in which you would give due consideration to the child's linguistic background, on admission to accommodation.

    What are the implications of your strategy for:

    a]   your organisation
    b]   your team
    c]   your own practice ?

Case example

A Chilean family, the Lopez, contact you via the health visitor, for services to help them with 3 year old Patricia, who has spina bifida. Already well known to health and education departments, Patricia attends a pre-school nursery 3 mornings a week and will go to the local special school at age 5. She has a 1 year old sister, Elena, and an elderly grandmother lives with them. The Lopez are political refugees and have lived in Britain for 12 years. They are now able to return to Chile for a visit. Mr and Mrs Lopez plan to go in a few months time for 6 weeks with Elena, but are unable to take Patricia who needs constant care. Mrs Lopez senior is unable to look after her. The family wonder whether a suitable foster family can be found to get to know Patricia with a view to looking after her for the 6 weeks.

7. CHILDREN WITH DISABILITIES

The extent of the changes

Children with disabilities who cannot live at home are placed in a much wider range of family and residential accommodation than their able-bodied counterparts, usually in order to make available to them specialist care and facilities. In most instances, the greater the disability, the more likely it is that this will become the overriding factor in placement suitability and availability. Some children live permanently away from home in boarding schools or hospitals or in private homes. Others need short term care because, for example, their carers need a holiday or are ill themselves.

Children in all these situations will be affected by the new duties and powers local authorities and others have towards them under the Children Act. (See chart at beginning of Chapter 4) There is potential for a vastly-improved service to all children with disabilities as a result of integrating them with other children under mainstream child care law and provision; even a minimalist approach can improve the health and development of some children and young people. There is also new scope for parents, other interested people and organisations to challenge local authorities and other agencies on their interpretation of the law.

Implications for practice

Placement with family or friends should be considered before placement with strangers. s.23(6)

In the case of a child with disabilities, this may mean being prepared to provide aids, adaptations and services under Part III to enable someone the child knows to be the carer. There are connections to be made here both with the availability of such resources and with the agency's charging policies if this means that expensive services are required and that parents will be liable to be charged.

Placement should be near home. s.23(7)

This is of particular importance to children who may be sent long distances to special residential establishments. Local authorities who are visiting these children will have to satisfy themselves that their welfare is being promoted by the placement, taking into account not just the children's special needs, but also the new requirements to work in partnership with family members and promote contact.(ss.85-87)

Placement should be with siblings. s. 23(7)

As above, this has implications for the placement being with a local, known carer; or it may be with a local foster carer or local residential establishment which would need adaptations or particular kinds of support to enable the placement to be successful.

The placement should be "not unsuitable to his particular needs". s.23(8)

This double negative seems to imply that local authorities and other agencies do not have to commit themselves to making a placement entirely suitable to the needs of a child with a disability; perhaps this is to avoid the possibility of legal action being taken against them if they are unable to provide homes which are suitably physically adapted for a particular child.

A more positive approach would be to seek accommodation which is:

i)   suitable in view of the child's race, culture, language, religion, class, gender, sexuality, family circumstances, the reasons for needing to be looked after, health and education needs and development;

ii)   suitable following consultation with the child, family and others;

iii)   physically suitable in respect of the child's disability;

iv)   emotionally suitable in terms of the carers' understanding of the child, the reasons for the child being looked after and of the disability;

v)   educationally suitable, both in respect of the child's abilities, and paying attention to the detrimental effect of too many moves.

Children themselves are to be consulted. s .20(6)

Whilst this should always have been so, it is firmly stressed throughout the legislation that their wishes and feelings are to be properly listened to and given due regard. Children with certain kinds of disability may have been particularly ignored or misunderstood, but practitioners will be expected to show how they have attempted to ascertain their views. It may be that there are other people better placed than the social worker making the placement to do this work, especially teachers, family members or friends.

In amongst the possibilities for improved services, however, are a few cautionary points:

The stigma of public care.

There is some concern that families who have had no previous dealings with social service departments may feel ashamed to have any contact with them, associating them with families who abuse their children; this may lead to a reluctance to accept any services and misunderstandings about why the authority is visiting their child in residential accommodation. The Department of Health's aim is that the new emphasis on working in partnership with parents and the retention of parental responsibility will dispel this. A positive approach to publicity and good rapport with other professionals will be essential in reassuring families, as will sensitive methods of collecting information for the register of "disabled children". (See Chapter 2)

The bureaucracy of official intervention.

Again, some families will have made satisfactory arrangements for the short-term care of their child which have involved little or no contact with the department. The introduction of new procedures set out in regulations for inspection, reviews and monitoring should be applied with this very much in mind, maintaining the flexibility and self sufficiency which families value so highly.

8)   Charging policies.

The Act says that all authorities must decide whether to charge for any of its services provided under Part III, except for advice, guidance and counselling. Most authorities do charge parents for accommodation, usually on a sliding scale, and usually with exemptions for those on low benefits. The Act does not allow those on income support or family credit to be charged. The implications for families with a child with disabilities are two-fold:

first, they may find themselves in a position where there is a choice of short-term accommodation for their child, e.g. in a distant hospital or with local foster carers, and they must accept the hospital bed against their wishes because it is free and the foster care is not;

secondly, many of these families are receiving benefits such as mobility or attendance allowance, or from 1992 the new Disability Living Allowance, if it gains parliamentary approval. They will need instant and expert welfare rights advice if they are to be charged, in case the charge levied by the local authority puts them below the income support level. The charging policy of the local authority may be such that the child's disability-related benefits are counted as part of the family's income and are therefore "available" to the authority. It can only do this if it is reasonable, and practitioners may want to challenge the introduction of such a policy.

Chapter 4

*Social Work
Agencies and
children who are
looked after*

ORGANISATION EXERCISE

*   How many children with disabilities live in your agency's area?

*   How many children with disabilities were being looked after by your organisation
during the past year?

*   What are the placement resources that you have available for children with different
kinds of disability? Are there gaps which have implications for new recruitment or the
reorganisation of existing provision?

*   Who will have responsibility for organising service for children with disabilities after
implementation of the Children Act? Who are your current specialists?

*   What are your agency's links (formal and informal) with other professionals, with
parents, self help groups, national advice agencies and others who are living with, or
directly involved with disabilities?

TEAM EXERCISE

*   **Using either a case example of your own, or the story of Patricia Lopez (p. 118),
divide   your team into 3 groups, who have the following tasks:**

i)   think up the most obstructive ways in which your team could respond to this request
for accommodation

ii)   list the ways in which your team would currently respond to the request

iii) devise a positive strategy for responding to the request.

**The whole team together then discuss ways to eliminate the obstructive practice, and
move forward from current practice to the response you would most like to see.**

What are the implications for:

-    the organisation
-    resource provision, including time, skills, placement options
-    staff attitudes, knowledge and training needs

VI.   ANTI-DISCRIMINATORY WORK WITH CHILDREN WHO ARE BEING LOOKED AFTER

The general duty of local authorities towards children who are looked after by them is shared by voluntary organisations and those running registered children's homes. It is to:

a)   safeguard and promote the welfare of the child, and

b)   make reasonable use of services which would be available to the child if living with her or his parents.

Within that context, it would be reasonable to assume that good practice towards these children should follow the Principles and Practice Guide points highlighted at the beginning of this chapter. (see p 86) The intention of the work is always to help the child grow into a healthy adult; for all parents and carers, this responsibility involves planning, juggling priorities, reviewing goals, making mistakes and learning from experience. Local authorities and other temporary carers of children are no exception, but the position of authority which they hold by virtue of their organisational status and legal powers means that they must carry out their duties towards children with especial care and wisdom.

Despite many good intentions, well thought out policies and even despite high resource provision, this is sadly not always the case, and there is too much research and anecdotal evidence to try to pretend that poor practice and poor planning for children is an occasional hiccup or rare misfortune:

Re. admissions to care -

"Over half the decisions were made within a week and more than a third were made within twenty four hours." (16)

"Too often this was conducted in a way calculated to reinforce rather than reduce the shock and damage of separation for the children and young people involved. Long established lessons of good child care practice were honoured more in the breach than in the observance. (17)

After admission -

" With a few notable exceptions, there is litle evidence to suggest that planning becomes any more prominent an activity as time progresses." (18)

"...It was rarely possible to pin-point when, or how, the decision that they would not return home had been taken." (19)

Readers will no doubt be able to think of many examples from their own experience, when their best efforts to work effectively against inequality with the children in their care have been hindered. The framework of the Children Act encourages the review of some of the issues, notably race and disability, but is silent on others, such as poverty, gender and sexual identity. In working with these children a positive approach to equality can be incorporated in many ways. In the remainder of this chapter, we will explore some of them.

4

Chapter

*Social Work
Agencies and
children who are
looked after*

These include:

1.   Working in partnership with children and young people.

2.   Promoting the positive and healthy development of a child's identity and self-esteem, and that of their parents to encourage their parenting

3.   Attending to the likely future needs of children when they are no longer in accommodation.

1. WORKING IN PARTNERSHIP WITH CHILDREN AND YOUNG PEOPLE

(a)   The nature and experience of discrimination

" I think partnership is a deceitful word, because partnership implies equality and there's no equality. A child does not have equal rights with an adult, by virtue of the fact that they haven't got the same experience." (interview for this book with Black and in Care)

" Maybe we need to suggest a different kind of word which they can use... which implies working together as positively as possible, which doesn't pretend that you've got equality in terms of decision making power or access to information... perhaps interdependent is a better word." (as above)

There is no doubt that children and their social workers are in an unequal relationship, due both to differences in age and experience and the power inherent in the worker's job and organisation. For some children there will be additional imbalances in respect of ethnicity, class, gender, sexual identity, physical and mental abilities. It is essential that workers recognise and accept that this power exists before attempting to address equality issues with children. Many workers, because of frustration and disillusionment feel that they are powerless within their organisation to effect any change, and can mistake this for a lack of real power in

relation to children and families. Their power derives from being part of a hugely-influential and interconnected system of local government, courts, schools, police and doctors backed up by extensive legal authority to make decisions about and for children. When this is put into the wider context of societal and national prejudice and inequality, it becomes clear how children living away from home in local authority and other accommodation are peculiarly vulnerable to any destructive, discriminatory use of their power by social workers.

It is not enough therefore, for workers to simply make a personal resolution to, for example, involve individual children more fully in decision-making forums, although this is a positive first step. This change must be supported by:

-    a rethinking of the relationship between the organisation and the child

-    a commitment to understand how the organisation can and does oppress the child, and

-    taking responsibility for trying to end that oppression.

For example:

A residential worker who is unhappy that children at her establishment are only allowed in at the end of their reviews, may try to negotiate on behalf of the children with whom she works closely. On further reflection, she may feel that the whole establishment operates in a way which rarely allows children's voices to be heard and that girls are heard less than boys. Depending on her own position within the staff group, the worker will need to decide whether, and at what level, to challenge the inequality; may initiate discussions about this sexism, about encouraging children to take more responsibility, about allowing independent advocates, about staff training needs and so on. She may decide to look outside the establishment, or even outside the agency for support and new ideas.

CHECKPOINT

* If you were in this kind of position, or have had a similar experience, what could you or did you do?

* What would be the pros and cons, both for you and the children, of different kinds of action you could take?

(b) Improving partnership skills

To participate in a decision-making process, children need the same basic foundation as adults; with this in place, they can develop the confidence to make an assertive contribution. This framework will need to comprise, amongst other things: information, the right to be consulted, the power to take action and support.

(b) 1 Information

There are three duties in the Children Act which demand that local authorities inform children, as well as adults, of certain provisions:

- one is in schedule 2(1), which refers to publishing information about services provided by them under Part III;

- the second is in section 26(8), which refers to the publicity about the representations and complaints procedures which are to be set up;

- the third is in section 26(2)(g) which requires that children being looked after are informed about any step which they may take under the Act.

Local authorities are expected to make this information not only available, but also accessible to those who may need it. (See Chapter 2) It is difficult to imagine how an authority could avoid the implication that each child being looked after, as well as each child in need and their representative, should have their own written information for reference. In addition, an imaginative authority may design posters and leaflets for distribution in schools, youth clubs, hostels and refuges, probation offices, libraries and any other place where young people meet.

CHECKPOINT

* what information is routinely given to children, and at what stage; is the information repeated as it may have been lost, forgotten or misunderstood (especially by people under stress); is there an assumption that someone else is doing it; is this checked at every review?

Apart from these statutory obligations, practitioners should routinely make available information about the rights children have to initiate, change or refuse to allow certain things to happen, as outlined below. Without such a commitment, children can easily lose their rights altogether.

There are many practitioners, in different organisations, whose job this could be. They include field and residential workers in local authorities and voluntary organisations, proprietors of residential establishments, boarding schools and hospitals, education social workers, intermediate treatment officers, solicitors, guardians *ad litem*, teachers and school counsellors, youth and community workers, hostel and refuge workers. The primary legal responsibility lies with the local authority, however, and so their staff must take the lead in reviewing existing procedures, updating current information and arranging joint training as necessary. It would be particularly helpful and constructive to make these plans together with children and young people currently being looked after, and those who have left accommodation, as the most effective way of ensuring that the right message gets across to children in the future.

(b) 2 Consultation

The Act contains five duties which are intended to ensure that children are properly consulted about what is happening in their lives at each important decision making stage. This applies not only to those involved with local authorities but also to children affected by private law proceedings.

- the most crucial of these is the s.1 duty that the courts, in every case before them, should ascertain the child's wishes and feelings. Some children who are being looked after will have been through a court process, perhaps leading to a care order; others will have had no court contact at all.

- secondly, all children must have been consulted before the accommodation is provided (s.20(6)); this extends to the police taking emergency action (s.46(3)).

- thirdly, all children being looked after must be consulted about any decision to be made (s.22(4))

- fourthly, they are to have their cases reviewed, and should have their views ascertained at each review (s.26(1))

- fifthly, they have the right to refuse medical examinations and other assessments, and therefore must be consulted about them (s.38(6),s.43(8), s.44(7))

(b) 3 The power to take action

Children and young people have rightly been suspicious of so-called consultation procedures which they feel have simply been another way of telling them what adults intend to do. They are well aware that, without proper information and advice, and a satisfactory forum for consultation, they are unable to exercise the rights they do have in a situation in which many of them feel powerless and frustrated. They also know that, unless they demand their rights, these are often ignored and local authorities fail in their statutory duties towards them.

It is crucial that children and young people are told about their new rights under the Children Act in a routine and straightforward way, which enables them to take further advice and action in time to exercise them.

Significant new rights include:

* the power to initiate certain court proceedings (private law orders under s.8)

* the power to refuse medical examinations or other assessments

* the power to use a local authority's representations and complaints procedure if they are a child in need

* the power, at age 16, to enter local authority accommodation without parental consent

* the power, at age 16 or 17, to request accommodation as a child in need whose welfare is likely to be seriously prejudiced

* the power to request advice and assistance from a local authority until age 21, under certain conditions.

(Not all these options are open to children being looked after; for example, the courts are not allowed to make a s.8 order on those already on care orders, although they can make a s.34 order)

Power to take action - implications for practice

There is no age bar to the first three powers above.
The Act has introduced no lower age limit on children who may exercise these powers (see s.4(4) s.10(8) s.38(6) s.43(8) s.44(7)). This means that it would be improper for an authority or any other agency to impose arbitrary age limits in guidance or policy regarding children they are looking after or advising. The key concept is the child's maturity to understand the consequences of the course of action they propose. This is an important

step for the rights of younger children to be heard.

Children must be "of sufficient understanding" to make their applications or refuse to consent to an examination or assessment. In the case of consent, these sections were introduced at a late stage in the Bill's passage through Parliament. They are based on the principle established in the Gillick case (Gillick v West Norfolk and Wisbech Area Health Authority [1986] AC112) that, as they grow older, children are more able, and should be allowed, to make informed decisions about their lives. This particular case involved teenagers and contraception, but as implementation takes effect, workers are likely to face situations of more complexity and delicacy. The law is quite clear that, as long as the child properly understands the purpose and procedure of the assessment, nobody can force her or him to undertake it; that includes parents, the local authority and the court. Social workers who feel strongly that an examination is crucial to a child's health and safety will be able to explain their concern to the court, but that does not absolve them of their duty to inform the child of their right to refuse, nor empower them to carry out the examination.

Social workers will need guidance, perhaps through training or discussion groups, to discuss possible scenarios. Those who are committed to working together with children and respect their right to make appropriate decisions, will no doubt welcome the support these provisions bring, but even these powers will be undermined without professional clarity about the meaning and extent of "sufficient understanding". It is likely to be a matter of months, or even years, before case law establishes satisfactory precedents, which means that social work must take the initiative, with the advice of colleagues, aboout possible criteria. This is especially important, for example, for children with communication problems, learning difficulties or behavioural disorders, and for children who do not speak English.

(b) 4 Support

Children being looked after need very particular kinds of support, over and above that needed by every child to promote their health, safety and development. These children, already experiencing situations and emotions of great stress, are additionally placed under a different kind of strain simply by being involved in the system of state care. This will be true even for those for whom removal from home was a relief, or at their own request, and despite feeling loved by their new carers. Many do not clearly understand why they are not living at home, are not fully aware of the problems to be resolved before they can return and have no idea of the time it will take. This uncertainty may be compounded by lack of contact with family and friends, movement to a new area or new school, interviews with strange adults and possibly police or medical examinations.

There are four ways in which the Children Act may assist towards children receiving greater support so that they are better able to participate as - admittedly unequal, but nevertheless, essential - partners:

[i] Greater contact with people they know. The duties to promote and sustain contact with family, friends and community will enable those whom children know best, to support them through their anxiety and uncertainty. Courts will be able to give directions for contact from the outset of proceedings, and in care proceedings will be obliged to consider what arrangements the authority is making for contact and invite comments from the parties on those arrangements. (s.34(11)) In a minority of cases of children being looked after, there will be a reduction or refusal of contact with a family member for safety reasons. Practitioners wanting to positively support their young partners will look to other family members, previous carers or friends who can give them this help instead. It may be, for example, that an older brother or sister, close cousin, ex-teacher or young person who was her or himself previously looked

after by the agency, will be appropriate.

[ii] Greater access to guardians ad litem

There is a wider range of court proceedings in which guardians will be appointed, reflecting the government's view that they should be appointed in over 90% of cases (20). This includes applications for a child assessment order or to discharge an emergency protection order. As children are to be allowed to refuse assessments if of "sufficient understanding" and can apply to discharge an emergency protection order, the role of the guardian will be crucial in determining the extent to which they are informed about, and decide whether to exert, these rights. Guardians will also be appointed when the local authority applies for authority to place a young person in secure accommodation.

[iii] Advocates for representations and complaints procedures

Children being looked after and other children in need may use a local authority's representations and complaints procedure. An example of the latter may be that of a 16 year old who is asking for accommodation against the wishes of his parents and has been refused. The D.o.H. draft guidance states that children being looked after: "*will need support at every stage if they are to be confident enough to invoke the procedure and to be sure that making a representation will not rebound upon them.*" (21). They suggest that someone not directly involved in the child's case should be made available to assist her or him. In addition, "*The complainant should also be informed of his right to be accompanied by another person who shall be entitled to be present at the whole meeting and to speak on his behalf if he so wishes.*" (Reg 10,3) Practitioners need to be open to encouraging a number of people to act in this capacity, not necessarily only those whom they know and are comfortable with. If a child needs an interpreter or assistance because of communication difficulties, this person should not replace the child's advocate. Such assistance should be automatically offered, free of charge.

[iv] Independent visitors

There is a power for local authorities to appoint independent visitors for children whom they are looking after, when communication between them and their parents is infrequent or they have not been visited by their parents for the previous 12 months. (sch.2(17)) This is a power with great potential to work for the benefit of children in boarding schools and other residential accommodation, who may see their social worker almost as infrequently as their parents. The extent to which it is used will depend on a generous interpretation of "infrequent" in order to promote contact for such children with others from outside of the care system. Young people and their advocates have continually stressed the importance and great value to them of having someone genuinely independent to talk to, and so the choice and appointment of the visitor must be undertaken with great care, and must always have the agreement of the child concerned. The ethnicity, gender and other characteristics of the visitor must be carefully considered in the light of the child's own needs and circumstances. The child has the right, if of sufficient understanding, to refuse the appointment of the visitor. This offers children the opportunity to identify a significant adult from their past and establish a recognised relationship with them, and it would be sensible to allow them as much choice in this matter as is possible.

2. PROMOTING THE POSITIVE AND HEALTHY DEVELOPMENT OF CHILDREN'S IDENTITY

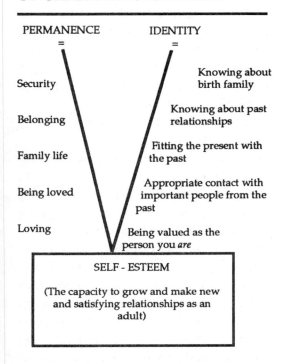

PERMANENCE = IDENTITY =

Security

Belonging

Family life

Being loved

Loving

Knowing about birth family

Knowing about past relationships

Fitting the present with the past

Appropriate contact with important people from the past

Being valued as the person you *are*

SELF - ESTEEM

(The capacity to grow and make new and satisfying relationships as an adult)

From: Child Placement by June Thoburn, 1989

The process

The active encouragement of a child's healthy emotional, intellectual and physical development is an essential component of the responsibility of any carer. Local authorities and others caring for children away from home have an additional responsibility which is to encourage a sense of self esteem and clear identity in children who are lacking the usual supports to enable this to grow. There are some children for whom this task is especially vital. They are those who face discrimination before they are placed in accommodation and who continue to face it whilst they are being looked after, unless deliberate action is taken to recognise and fight the prejudice which damages them.

The purpose of any action would be to:

- assess and record all aspects of the child's identity and circumstances,

- note gaps in that information and

check assumptions,

- assess whether the child faces any discrimination as a result of that identity,

- allocate workers to deal with actual or potential discrimination, and

- review the work at statutory reviews.

This assessment, work and review process should involve the children as far as possible, particularly in enabling them to voice their experiences of prejudice and be heard with respect, and to have their views about it to be taken into account. (s.22 duty to continue to consult, and continue to take into account race, culture, religion and language). The responsibility for tackling the discrimination, however, lies entirely with the organisation, and not with the child.

CHECKPOINT

* How far does your agency currently undertake this kind of work with children being looked after by you?

* Where are the gaps, and what can be done to change procedures to promote positive action on this issue?

* To what extent is your agency willing to undertake full monitoring of children's needs along these lines? If they are not, how do you demonstrate that you are taking all the relevant circumstances into account when making decisions about them and promoting their welfare?

If an agency wanted to initiate such full scale monitoring, and apply it to a wide range of issues, what would usefully be covered? :

- race, culture, religion, language and disability are already covered by the Children Act and are therefore statutory requirements;

Chapter 4

*Social Work
Agencies and
children who are
looked after*

- gender, sexual identity, class and poverty are not covered.

Let us take one example from this second list and highlight some issues:

Sexual identity

a) *Organisational responsibility*

There is no mention in legislation, and very little in social work texts, about the sexual identity of any social work client. There is an assumption of heterosexuality amongst both staff and clients, despite research which indicates that between 10% and 20% of the population are lesbian or gay. (22)(23) Taking the lower figure as a guide, together with the numbers of children in care in England and Wales in the year ending March 1988: 64,352 (24) means there are approximately 6,435 children and young people being looked after by local authorities who may become lesbian or gay adults.

Within authorities and voluntary social work agencies, there are rarely any policy statements or objectives which are precisely anti-heterosexist *(see glossary)*. Those which do exist tend to focus on the recruitment of lesbian and gay foster carers. On the whole, good practice is localised and unsupported by formal policy guidelines. What is unique about this form of discrimination is that it is still considered acceptable in some areas to express disgust, contempt, hatred and pity towards people solely on the basis of their sexual identity. It is also possible in this country, and happens particularly in work with children, to sack staff for being lesbian or gay. Public, organisational and union complacency about such behaviour is rarely challenged. When a team does develop a positive policy, for example as in the experience of the fostering and adoption unit in the London Borough of Waltham Forest, the workers involved and their managers were exposed to fierce criticism and pressure to withdraw, despite eventually receiving a positive mandate from the full Council to continue.

Situations like this, with their painful consequences for workers, carers and children should by now be inexcusable in social work services. The profession should, through its own education and management processes, have successfully challenged such bigotry. Its failure to do so has resulted in a lesbian and gay workforce which must, by and large, conceal its identity, at great cost both to itself, to clients and to colleagues.

b) *Young people's experience of discrimination*

Of approximately 64,000 children being looked after, many have undeveloped sexuality, many believe that they are heterosexual and many will have emotional and sexual attachments to people of both sexes during their adolescence and adulthood. There are a number, however, who are aware of their lesbian or gay identity at an early age and, like their contemporaries in wider society, begin early on to suffer from the hostility and fear which is a widespread reaction to this knowledge. These youngsters experience great isolation; they cannot tell families and friends; they pretend to be something they're not; they have no role models; they are given an unrelenting message in the media that what they are and how they feel is deeply wrong. The damaging effect on their emotional health, their sense of self and emerging adult identity can be profound.

"We've had lesbian and gay young people phone up... who have been bullied, abused and everything because they are gay. We now recognise that it is a big problem." (Naypic)

Some find it such a big problem that they run away from their carers to live on the streets.

"In the spring of 1989, 16 year old Albert Kennedy fell to his death from the top of Chorlton Street car park in the centre of Manchester. Albert was a male prostitute, a runaway from the 'care' of - social services.
On the night of his death, Albert was with his 19 year old boyfriend; he was depressed and had

taken a tab of LSD for the first time. They had sought the safety of Chorlton Street car park to escape a car load of 'queerbashers'. Unable to talk Albert out of his depressed 'trip', his boyfriend had gone down for help. The next he saw of Albert was his dead body covered with a blanket." (Scene Out June 1989)

A trust was set up in Albert's name to help homeless young lesbians and gay young men or those who are living in unsupportive or threatening homes. The Trust volunteers recruit lesbian and gay "big sisters and big brothers" to provide accommodation and positive role models for them.

c)   *How to develop positive practice with young lesbians and gay men*

The most immediate problem facing workers who want to help these youngsters is to identify them. Clearly, monitoring of sexual identity, in the same way as, for example, ethnicity is neither practicable nor desirable. However, there are many practice ideas which could go a long way to safeguard and promote their immediate and future welfare. These are just a few:

i)   put across clear messages which let young people know that not everyone is heterosexual and that it is equally valid to be lesbian, gay or heterosexual;

ii)   ensure that publicity is given to positive role models;

iii)   challenge heterosexist behaviour and language by workers, children and other adults;

iv)   find information about local and national groups, helplines and meeting places; publicise these in offices, residential homes and so on;

v)   arrange for anti- heterosexism training for staff, foster carers and prospective adopters and include positive work on this during the assessment process;

vi)   identify social work staff, counsellors or youth workers who are willing and able to talk to young people about their sexual identity, and ensure that they know how to contact them in confidence;

vii)   do not neglect children living far from the area in residential establishments. They are in particular need of good, supportive information and literature;

viii)   there are many lesbians and gay men with disabilities, and young people need to know how to contact their specialist organisations;

ix)   check your local library for good lesbian and gay literature and add it to the bookshelves in your office, centre or home and make then available to foster carers and adopters; and

x)   be aware of the importance of proactive work in this area. Policy or practice which intends to be neutral or non-judgemental will invariably be perceived by young lesbians and gay men as negative as they will assume it reflects the hostile messages they receive from elsewhere.

Chapter 4

Social Work Agencies and children who are looked after

3. ATTENDING TO THE LIKELY FUTURE NEEDS OF CHILDREN AND YOUNG PEOPLE

Local authority duties and powers

There was considerable pressure on the government to strengthen local authorities' responsibilities towards young people who leave their care, especially from the age of 16 onwards. The result is s.24, which does not go as far as many had wished, and which is felt to be necessary to force some authorities to take seriously their parenting duties. (25)

The Act states:
" Where a child is being looked after by a local authority, it shall be the duty of the authority to advise, assist and befriend him with a view to promoting his welfare when he ceases to be looked after by them" (s.24(1))

Young people who qualify have to:

- be over 16 and under 21

- have been accommodated by a local authority or other organisation, or privately fostered between the ages of 16 and 17

- appear to the authority to be in need of advice and being befriended

- and that the person by whom they were being looked after does not have the necessary resources to advise and befriend them. (s.24(2)(3)(4)(5))

The local authority has the power to give this assistance in kind or, exceptionally, in cash (s.24(7) and to contribute towards expenses incurred by young people whom the authority was looking after in finding and keeping employment or training.(s.24(8))

There is also a power to charge young people for services provided except for assistance in connection with employment, education or training (s.24(10))

CHECKPOINT

* What provision does your agency make currently for young people who are no longer being looked after by you?

These are some of the issues which will make a difference to the ways in which these duties and powers are carried out:

a) Connection to the welfare duty

Arrangements for children and young people who are about to leave an agency's accommodation and live independently, cannot begin only 6 months, or even a year before they leave. Workers who take seriously the need for anti-discriminatory practice at earlier stages in children's lives will be aware of how crucial it is when they reach adolescence and are striving for independence. Some of the areas to pay attention to include:

* developing a strong sense of racial, cultural and religious identity and pride, including knowledge of wider heritage, family memories; personal affiliation; positive images of own ethnic group; connections with others from same ethnic group and local community;

* maintaining links with family, friends and own community, and forging new links in the area to which they are to move; and

* developing a positive image of self, including gender, sexuality, different abilities.

Unless this groundwork takes place over the whole period during which children are being looked after, then it will become especially hard for them to move into adulthood with confidence and necessary survival skills.

b) The meaning of "advise, assist and befriend"

How are local authorities to intepret these words? They may well have a hollow ring to them for many young people who have felt abandoned by their social workers as soon as they have left their care. They are really not strong enough to give the impetus to bureaucratically structured authorities to behave as reasonable parents in providing for growing young adults, and appear to let them off the hook of this responsibility by trying to imply that, at this stage, they have a more equal relationship with them. It is extremely questionable, however, how far a social worker can be seen to be the friend of a young person in this position, when the worker has all the power, especially the money, and also has the ability to walk away from the '"friendship" by leaving her or his job.

c) Providing support

Amongst the priorities of all care leavers' list of needs must be a support network to establish themselves in the world:

"The most important aspect of leaving care is the loneliness. When I needed help most was 6 months after I left care when all the dreams turned out to be false" (Sue Brazier, Who Cares? Magazine, NCB)

One project which may have helped Sue and others like her, is the "Care Free" centre, funded by the London Borough of Southwork . It is open on a drop-in basis 2.5 days a week for specialist advice and friendship, offering women's groups, black groups and training courses.

It is an example of how much this part of the Act is going to depend heavily on authorities' willingness to allocate funding to provide appropriate resources. Support for youngsters no longer being looked after is unlikely to feature highly on any authority's list of the services which cannot be reduced. What these young people clearly lack, though, is the kind of support network which children growing up within their

own families are more likely to have, with the kind of experience, knowledge, helping hands and discipline which that implies. This may improve over time if authorities respond to other duties in the Act to sustain links between children and their families, or appoint independent visitors; given the level of estrangement between many teenagers away from home and their parents it will be vital to seek out other adults who can bridge those gaps.

d) Money

16 and 17 year olds moving towards independence are not catered for in our current system of state maintenance, which assumes that all young people in this age group are living at home with their parents and financially dependent on them, are at work or are in full time education or training. To get income support, a young person has to be in very strictly defined circumstances, such as a single parent or disabled, or be classed as in "severe hardship". Many fail to qualify at all, or don't want to submit to humiliating interviews. Even if they do qualify, the rates of benefit work against independent living. If they do approach or are taken to a local authority, they may be covered by the duties towards children in need.

It is important for local authorities to acknowledge, when planning the allocation of resources for young people, that the duties under s.24 operate retrospectively. Therefore young people for whom the authority was responsible under previous legislation are entitled, up to 21 years, to seek assistance.

It is possible to envisage a great deal of negotiating between inner city boroughs and their counterparts in the country, when those "picking up" these young people look to recoup their costs from originating authorities. In 1989, Centrepoint (a shelter for homeless young people in central London) found that 75% of those using the night shelter were from outside London. They were therefore additionally disadvantaged by their lack of local connections and knowledge.

Local authorities will need to have very clear strategies for dealing with requests for

Chapter 4

Social Work Agencies and children who are looked after

help under this section; in particular, they will have to define "exceptional circumstances". It seems inevitable that, as a result of the denial of benefit to these young people, they will in fact, fall within exceptional circumstances very easily. Should this cover, for example, advance rent deposits, without which accommodation cannnot be obtained?

e) Housing

The Centrepoint survey also found that one third of its clients had been in the care of a local authority, which indicates a serious inability on the part of social work agencies to adequately parent this age group. It also highlights again the need for a corporate strategy and sense of accountability which would see housing, education and social service departments working together to provide suitable transitional arrangements for those moving to independence.

TEAM EXERCISE

*   Under what circumstances do you think it would be reasonable to make a payment to a young person under s.24(7)? Invite a group of young people in to discuss this with you. Can you make their views known to your managers and elected members who are devising your criteria?

*   What is the minimum level of support that you think your team should be providing to young people who leave your accommodation? What do they think? - What links do you have with the voluntary sector who work with young people in, or from, your area?

*   Do you know the benefit entitlements of different groups of young people, depending on their age, any disability or other circumstances? If not, see if someone can advise you so that you have this information ready.

*Social Work
Agencies and
children who are
looked after*

1) Provision for children in need of boarding or residential education
E. Anderton & A Morgan
Boarding Schools Association 1987

2) Networks Video
London Borough of Islington. Social Services Training Section 1987

3) Permanency planning for children
A.Maluccio, E.Fein, K.Olmstead, Tavistock 1986

4) Using written agreements with children and families
Family Rights Group, 1989

5) as above, no.2

6) as above, Chapter 1 no.34

7) as above, no.2

8) as above, no.2

9) Issues of race and culture in the family placement of children
(letter to directors of social service departments from SSI)
D.o.H 1990

10) Finding black families for black children in care; a case study
E.Arnold and M.James in New Community 15(3) pp.417-425 1989

11) Practice note 18:
Recruiting Black Families
British Agencies for Adoption and Fostering 1991

12) as above, Chapter 3 no.17

13) as above, no.9

14) The boarding out of children
(foster placement)
regulations 1988, No.5(4)

15) as above, no.9

16) Who needs care?
Social work decisions about children
J.Packman et al. Blackwell 1986

17) as above, no.16

18) In care - a study of social work decision making
J. Vernon and D. Fruin NCB 1985

19) as above, no.18

20) H.C. Deb, 23 May 1989,
Standing Committee B, col.255 from R.White el al: A guide to the Children Act 1989
Butterworths 1989

21) as above, Chapter 2 no.9

22) Sexual behaviour in the human female
A. Kinsey, 1953

23) Social work and the invisible minority: an exploration of lesbianism
S.Potter and T. Darty in Social Work USA, Vol.26(3) 1981

24) Children in care of local authorities
(year ending 31 March 1988)
Government Statistical Service, D.o.H.   1991

25) Care leaver's guide plus training pack on the Children Act
Who cares? magazine, NCB forthcoming

Chapter 4

*Social Work
Agencies and
children who are
looked after*

FURTHER READING
SUGGESTIONS

1) **A chance for gay people**
D. Smart in Community Care
24/01/91

2) **Children in lesbian and single
parent households:**
psychosexual and psychiatric
appraisal
Golombok et al. 1983

3) **Sticks and carrots - using the Race
Relations Act to remove bad practice
and the Children Act to promote good
practice**
J. Lane in Local Government Policy
Making vol.17 No.3 Dec.1990

4) **Practice with care**
A.Ahmad, REU 1990

5) **Ethnic sensitive social work
practice**
W.Devore and E.Schlesinger, Merrill
1987

6) **Video: Coffee coloured children**
A non-aligned production. Albany
Video Distribution 1988

7) **Practice guide for social workers on
the placement of black children in
care.**
BASW 1987

CONCLUSION

In developing the ideas in this guide, the Steering Group set out to begin to make anti-racist and anti-discriminatory practice central to all child care and child protection practice undertaken under the Children Act 1989.

The book represents our thoughts on how to move forward. It is not intended to be the final or definitive statement on the subject. We see the guide as the starting point for action, which we believe must be taken by managers and practitioners in consultation with service users.

If you want to use the opportunity offered by the Children Act to make a difference to the quality and standard of child care provision in the 1990s, you must take that action now.